Livs
Happy Cooking!
Love Gru xxx
March 2022

THE

JACKFRUIT
COOKBOOK

HEATHER THOMAS

THE
JACKFRUIT
COOKBOOK

HEATHER THOMAS

EBURY
PRESS

CONTENTS

MAIN MEALS

DESSERTS, PRESERVES & DRINKS

INTRODUCTION

A quiet revolution is going on in our eating habits. Vegetarian and vegan foods have gone mainstream and we're all eating less meat and more plant proteins. This trend is here to stay as more people want a healthier, greener and more sustainable lifestyle.

Jackfruit is the versatile, healthy fruit with a 'meaty' texture that has cornered the vegetarian and vegan market. You can buy it fresh, canned (in brine, water or syrup), frozen, dried, or cleaned and ready to cook in vacuum-packed pouches in many supermarkets, health food stores, delis and specialist Asian stores.

WHAT IS JACKFRUIT?

Jackfruit might be a new food trend in the West but it's been around for centuries in India. The evergreen jackfruit trees, along with figs, mulberries and breadfruit, are part of the *Moraceae* family native to the tropical regions of South East Asia, Africa and Brazil. They are drought- and pest-resistant, easy to cultivate and produce very high-yield crops, making them environmentally friendly.

Jackfruits can grow to an enormous size – up to 1 metre (3 feet) long with a weight of 40kg (88lb)! The mild unripe fruit is used in savoury dishes, where it absorbs the flavours of marinades, sauces, spices and seasonings. The ripe fruit is naturally sweet and scented and is used in desserts, baking, preserves and drinks.

HEALTH BENEFITS

Jackfruit is low in fat and is a good source of vitamins B6 and C, potassium and dietary fibre. And with only 20 calories (kcals) per 75g (2 ½ oz) and 40 per cent fewer carbs than rice and four times the fibre, it's a very healthy food. Plus, unlike other 'faux meats', it's soy- and gluten-free. It is also rich in phytochemicals and antioxidants, which play an important role in protecting us against cancer.

VERSATILITY

What makes jackfruit so special is its versatility – it can be cooked and served in so many ways. Use the young, green jackfruit, with its meaty texture, as a filling for tacos, burritos and pitta; stir-fry it with Thai flavourings; slow-cook it in stews and chilli; make it into burgers, patties and fritters; or add it to salads and slaws.

Ripe jackfruit is deliciously sweet, with a fragrance that's reminiscent of pineapple, mango and banana. You can blitz it in smoothies, shakes and juices; add it to fresh fruit salads; purée it for ice cream, sorbets and popsicles; bake it in muffins, cakes and bread; or make it into jam and preserves.

WHICH SORT SHOULD I USE?

If you're cooking savoury dishes you need to use the young, green jackfruit, which is almost flavourless and creamy white inside. You can also buy it canned, frozen or vacuum-packed in pouches.

For desserts, drinks, baking, smoothies and jam, use the ripe, sweet jackfruit. You'll know when a fresh jackfruit is ripe due to its intense aroma. When you cut it open, the edible pods will be yellow. Sweet, ripe jackfruit is also available canned, vacuum-packed and frozen.

PREPARING YOUNG, GREEN JACKFRUIT

1 Before you start, lubricate your hands and the knife with vegetable oil (or you can wear gloves), as the jackfruit pods are coated with sticky natural latex.

2 Cut the jackfruit in half lengthways and remove the central core. This will enable you to release the edible pods (arils).

3 Cut out the pods, discarding the fibrous strands wrapped around them.

4 Make a slit down one side of each pod and remove the stone (pit) and its rubbery casing.

5 You can now cook the pods or freeze them.

Note: Prepare ripe, sweet jackfruit in the same way. The pods will be ready to cook or to eat raw.

USING CANNED GREEN JACKFRUIT IN WATER OR BRINE

This is ready-prepared, so just drain and rinse the jackfruit in a sieve or colander under cold running water. Drain well and gently squeeze out any excess liquid. Pat dry with kitchen paper (paper towels). Depending on the recipe, you can use the jackfruit pieces (triangles) whole, or remove and discard the hard pointed ends before slicing the pieces or shredding them.

Note: It's a good idea to deseed the canned jackfruit for 'faux meat' recipes as the seeds don't shred well, but they are edible and you can cook them along with the fruit if wished.

USING CANNED SWEET, RIPE JACKFRUIT IN SYRUP

Drain the jackfruit, keeping or discarding the syrup according to the recipe. Follow the recipe instructions.

SNACKS

JACKFRUIT CHIPS

VEGAN

SERVES: 4 | **PREP:** 10 MINUTES | **COOK:** 5 MINUTES

350g/12oz prepared raw
   young, green jackfruit
   (see page 11)
vegetable oil, for deep-frying
1 tsp hot chilli powder
sea salt, for sprinkling

You need fresh, raw, firm-fleshed young green jackfruit to make these crispy golden chips. You can often find it ready-prepared and bagged up in Asian markets and some health food stores. Jackfruit chips are a really popular snack in southern India, especially Kerala, where the jackfruit trees grow wild and nearly every back yard has one.

1 Cut the raw fruit into long thin chip-shaped sticks. Remember to oil the knife blade and your hands or wear gloves when you do this due to the sticky latex on the jackfruit.

2 Heat the oil in a deep fryer or heavy saucepan until it reaches 190°C/375°F – you can check this with a thermometer, or try frying a small bread cube. When it's golden and crisp, the oil is ready.

3 Add the jackfruit chips to the hot oil in batches and deep-fry for at least 5 minutes until crisp and golden brown. Remove with a slotted spoon and drain on kitchen paper (paper towels). Keep warm while you cook the remaining chips in the same way.

4 Dust the chips with the chilli powder and sprinkle with sea salt. Eat immediately while crisp and piping hot.

NOTE:
You cannot make these chips with canned, frozen or pouched jackfruit – it must be unripe and fresh.

OR YOU CAN TRY THIS...
– Dust the hot chips with some cayenne pepper, paprika or ground turmeric.
– In Kerala, the chips are often fried in coconut oil, which gives them a distinctive flavour and aroma.

JACKFRUIT 'BACON' WITH AVOCADO TOAST

SERVES: 4 | **PREP:** 15 MINUTES | **CHILL:** 15-30 MINUTES | **COOK:** 20-25 MINUTES

400g/14oz can green
    jackfruit in brine,
    drained and rinsed
2 medium avocados, peeled,
    stoned (pitted) and
    coarsely mashed
juice of 1 lime
4 slices sourdough bread
sea salt and freshly ground
    black pepper
snipped chives, to garnish

For the spicy marinade:
2 tbsp molasses sugar
1 tsp ground cumin
1 tsp hot chilli powder
½ tsp sweet smoked paprika
1 tbsp aminos (liquid smoke)
1 tsp olive oil
1 tsp balsamic vinegar
1 tsp maple syrup

This is the perfect dish for vegetarians and vegans who miss crispy bacon. Eat it as a snack or for breakfast or brunch. You can make double the quantity of bacon and leave it to cool before storing in a sealed container in the fridge. Use in sandwiches and salads and for topping baked jacket potatoes.

1 Preheat the oven to 190°C, 375°F, gas mark 5. Line a baking tray (cookie sheet) with baking parchment.

2 Gently squeeze any excess water out of the jackfruit and pat dry with kitchen paper (paper towels). Cut each triangle horizontally into thin slices, so you end up with several triangles. Pat again with kitchen paper.

3 Put the spicy marinade ingredients into a bowl and mix well. Add the jackfruit and turn the slices gently in the marinade until coated all over. Chill in the fridge for 15–30 minutes.

4 Arrange the marinated jackfruit on the lined baking tray. Bake for 20–25 minutes, or until crisp and golden brown, turning the jackfruit halfway through.

5 Meanwhile, mix the mashed avocado with the lime juice and season with salt and pepper to taste.

6 Toast the bread and cover with the mashed avocado. Top with the hot crispy jackfruit 'bacon' and serve immediately, sprinkled with chives.

OR YOU CAN TRY THIS...

– Use brown sugar instead of molasses sugar in the marinade.
– Vary the spices, depending on how much heat you want.
– Sprinkle with chopped coriander (cilantro) or parsley.
– Serve with roasted or griddled baby plum tomatoes.

JACKFRUIT LOADED SWEET POTATO FRIES

SERVES: 4-6 | **PREP:** 10 MINUTES | **COOK:** 35-45 MINUTES

2 x 400g/14oz cans green
    jackfruit in brine, drained
    and rinsed
1 tbsp coconut oil
2 garlic cloves, crushed
1 tsp ground cumin
1 tsp chilli powder
½ tsp sweet smoked paprika
¼ tsp salt
120ml/4fl oz (½ cup)
    barbecue sauce
1 tbsp soy or tamari sauce
100g/3½oz (1 cup) grated
    Cheddar cheese

For the sweet potato fries:
500g/1lb 2oz sweet potatoes,
    washed and scrubbed
olive oil spray
good pinch of sea salt flakes
freshly ground black pepper
fresh herbs for sprinkling,
    e.g. rosemary or thyme
    leaves

A platter of crisp sweet potato fries topped with spicy pulled barbecue jackfruit and melted cheese is great for snacking on or serving with drinks before supper.

1 Preheat the oven to 180°C, 350°F, gas mark 4.

2 Make the sweet potato fries. Cut the sweet potatoes into long, thin matchsticks. Spread them out on a large baking tray (cookie sheet) and spray lightly with oil. Sprinkle with sea salt, black pepper and herbs. Bake in the oven for 30–40 minutes until crisp and golden brown.

3 Meanwhile, cut each piece of jackfruit into 3–4 slices, discarding the seeds.

4 Heat the coconut oil in a saucepan set over a medium heat and cook the garlic for 1–2 minutes without browning. Add the jackfruit, spices and salt and stir well until the jackfruit is coated in the spices. Cook, stirring occasionally, until the jackfruit is golden brown.

5 Reduce the heat to a simmer and add the barbecue and soy or tamari sauces. Cook gently for 15 minutes, then shred the jackfruit with 2 forks.

6 Arrange the sweet potato fries on a heatproof plate and top with the shredded jackfruit. Sprinkle the Cheddar over the top and pop under a hot grill (broiler) for 3–5 minutes until the cheese melts.

OR YOU CAN TRY THIS...
– Sprinkle the fries and jackfruit with chopped spring onions (scallions), sweetcorn kernels, black beans or kidney beans.
– Use grated mozzarella instead of Cheddar.
– Top with guacamole and sour cream.

JACKFRUIT 'CARNITAS' WITH FRUITY SALSA

SERVES: 4 | **PREP:** 15 MINUTES | **COOK:** 15-20 MINUTES

2 x 400g/14oz cans green
  jackfruit in brine, drained
  and rinsed
2 tbsp olive oil
1 red onion, finely chopped
4 garlic cloves, crushed
1 green jalapeño pepper,
  diced
1 tbsp dark soy sauce
2 tsp demerara sugar
1 tsp ground cumin
½ tsp sweet smoked paprika
good pinch of cayenne
¼ tsp salt
8 small soft tortillas

For the fruity salsa:
4 spring onions (scallions),
  chopped
2 green jalapeño peppers,
  deseeded and diced
450g/1lb ripe tomatoes,
  chopped
115g/4oz fresh pineapple,
  diced
juice of 1 lime
a handful of coriander
  (cilantro), chopped

This is a quick and easy way to make crispy jackfruit 'carnitas' without roasting them at the end in a hot oven. If you like really spicy food, try adding some chilli powder, ground chipotle or hot smoked paprika.

1 Make the fruity salsa: mix all the ingredients together in a bowl and set aside.

2 Pat the jackfruit dry with kitchen paper (paper towels) and then cut down through the core into thin slices. Gently squeeze dry once more with kitchen paper. The slices must be as dry as possible so that they'll crisp up when you cook them.

3 Heat 1 tablespoon of the oil in a large frying pan (skillet) set over a medium heat. Add the onion, garlic and jalapeño and cook, stirring occasionally, for 6–8 minutes until tender and golden.

4 Reduce the heat to low and stir in the jackfruit and soy sauce. Cook gently, stirring often, for at least 5 minutes until the mixture seems quite dry and no longer moist. Shred the jackfruit with a fork and add the rest of the oil together with the sugar, spices and salt. Cook for about 5 minutes, or until the jackfruit caramelizes and turns golden brown and crispy.

5 Meanwhile, heat the tortillas by dry-frying them for 1–2 minutes on each side in a clean frying pan, or by warming in a low oven.

6 Spoon the crispy jackfruit mixture onto the tortillas and roll them up. Serve immediately with the fruity salsa.

OR YOU CAN TRY THIS...
– Use the spicy jackfruit mixture as a filling for burritos and enchiladas.
– Add some mashed avocado or guacamole and salad to the tortillas.
– Serve with vegan cashew cream or, if you're not vegan, sour cream or yoghurt.

LOADED JACKFRUIT & GUACAMOLE NACHOS

SERVES: 4 | **PREP:** 15 MINUTES | **COOK:** 15 MINUTES

400g/14oz can green
   jackfruit in brine,
   drained, rinsed and
   shredded
400g/14oz can kidney
   beans, rinsed and drained
225g/8oz (1½ cups) hot
   salsa or pico de gallo
225g/8oz lightly salted corn
   tortilla chips
4 pickled jalapeños, thinly
   sliced
100g/3½oz (1 cup) grated
   Cheddar cheese
1 bunch of spring onions
   (scallions), thinly sliced
a few sprigs of coriander
   (cilantro), chopped
150g/5oz (1 cup) chunky
   guacamole

Nachos make a delicious snack, or you can serve them with pre-dinner drinks. Adding jackfruit to the hot salsa makes it more substantial and 'meaty'. For a vegan take on this dish, use shredded vegan cheese – you can buy brands that melt well and taste very similar to the real thing.

1 Preheat the oven to 200°C, 400°F, gas mark 6.

2 Mix the jackfruit, kidney beans and salsa or pico de gallo together in a bowl.

3 Put the tortilla chips in a large ovenproof dish and spoon the jackfruit mixture over the top. Sprinkle with the jalapeños and grated cheese.

4 Bake in the oven for about 15 minutes, or until the jackfruit is hot and the cheese is melted and bubbling.

5 Sprinkle the spring onions and coriander over the top and add some spoonfuls of guacamole. Serve immediately.

OR YOU CAN TRY THIS...
– Instead of pickled jalapeños, use 2 sliced fresh chillies.
– Use grated Monterey Jack cheese instead of Cheddar.
– Add a dollop of sour cream before serving.

CURRIED JACKFRUIT & SPINACH SAMOSAS VEGAN

MAKES: 8 | **PREP:** 30 MINUTES | **COOK:** 30-35 MINUTES

450g/1lb sweet potatoes, peeled and cubed
1 tbsp sunflower oil, plus extra for brushing
1 onion, finely chopped
2 garlic cloves, crushed
1 fresh red chilli, diced
1 tsp grated fresh root ginger
2 tsp black mustard seeds
1 tbsp curry paste
400g/14oz can green jackfruit in brine, drained, rinsed and shredded
200g/7oz baby spinach leaves
2 tbsp water
8 sheets vegan filo (phyllo) pastry
salt and freshly ground black pepper

These spicy samosas are oven-baked rather than fried in oil. Eat as a snack or serve as a light lunch with mango chutney, a cooling vegan cucumber raita and some salad or chapatis.

1 Preheat the oven to 200°C, 400°F, gas mark 6. Line a baking tray (cookie sheet) with baking parchment.

2 Cook the sweet potatoes in a saucepan of boiling water for about 10 minutes until just tender but not mushy. Drain well.

3 Meanwhile, heat the oil in a pan set over a low heat and cook the onion and garlic, stirring occasionally, for 6–8 minutes until softened. Add the chilli, ginger and mustard seeds and cook for 2 minutes until the seeds pop. Stir in the curry paste and cook for 1 minute.

4 Add the jackfruit, spinach and water and cook for 5 minutes. Stir in the cooked sweet potato and season to taste. Set aside to cool.

5 Place one sheet of filo pastry on a clean surface and brush lightly with oil. Cover with another sheet and brush that with oil. Cut lengthways down the middle into 2 long rectangles.

6 Place a spoonful of the cooled curry mixture on the top right-hand corner of each strip of pastry. Fold the pastry over the filling at an angle to make a triangle, then keep on folding it over until you get to the bottom of each strip. You should end up with a neat triangular pastry parcel enclosing the filling. Repeat with the remaining sheets of filo pastry and curry mixture to make 8 samosas.

7 Brush the samosas lightly with oil and place on the lined baking tray. Cook in the oven for 20–25 minutes until crisp and golden.

OR YOU CAN TRY THIS...
– Substitute frozen peas for the spinach.
– Add some cumin seeds and a pinch of ground turmeric.

JACKFRUIT VIETNAMESE SPRING ROLLS

MAKES: 8 | **PREP:** 20 MINUTES | **COOK:** 15-20 MINUTES

400g/14oz can green
   jackfruit in brine,
   drained and rinsed
60ml/2fl oz (¼ cup) hoisin
   sauce
2 tbsp soy or tamari sauce
1 tbsp rice vinegar
1 tbsp brown sugar
1 tbsp sesame oil
2 red (bell) peppers,
   deseeded and diced
1 large carrot, cut into
   small, thin matchsticks
2cm/1in piece fresh root
   ginger, peeled and diced
100g/3½oz spring greens,
   kale or spinach, shredded
100g/3½oz beansprouts
4 tbsp soy sauce
a handful of coriander
   (cilantro), chopped
8 round rice paper wrappers
satay sauce, for dipping

These spring rolls are fresher-tasting and healthier than fried ones.
You can make them ahead and keep them in a sealed container in the
fridge for 24 hours. Rice paper wrappers are available online and in
Asian stores, delis and many supermarkets.

1 Cut the jackfruit into slices and mix in a bowl with the hoisin sauce,
soy or tamari sauce, vinegar and sugar.

2 Heat the sesame oil in a wok or large frying pan (skillet) set over a
high heat. Stir-fry the red peppers, carrot and ginger for 2 minutes,
then add the greens and beansprouts and stir-fry for 2 minutes.
Stir in the 4 tbsp soy sauce and the coriander. Remove from the pan
and set aside until cold.

3 Reduce the heat to low and add the jackfruit mixture. Cook gently,
stirring often, for at least 5 minutes until the mixture seems quite
dry and no longer moist. Shred the jackfruit with a fork and cook
for 5–10 minutes more, or until the jackfruit starts to turn golden
brown and crispy. Set aside to cool.

4 Fill a bowl with cold water and position it near you while you assemble the spring rolls. Dip a rice paper wrapper into the water until it's pliable. Lay it out flat on a clean work surface and spoon some of the jackfruit and vegetable filling onto it, leaving a broad edge around it.

5 Fold the sides of the wrapper over the filling to enclose it, then roll it up like a parcel. Repeat with the rest of the wrappers and filling. Serve with satay sauce for dipping.

OR YOU CAN TRY THIS...

– Add some rice vermicelli – follow the directions on the packet and mix into the filling.
– Instead of coriander, use Thai basil or mint.
– Serve drizzled with sweet chilli sauce or sprinkled with soy sauce.

SPICY JACKFRUIT BITES

SERVES: 4 | **PREP:** 15 MINUTES | **MARINATE:** 15 MINUTES | **COOK:** 10-12 MINUTES

1 tbsp soy sauce
1 tbsp agave syrup
½ tsp garlic powder
2 x 400g/14oz cans green
   jackfruit in brine, drained
   and rinsed
vegetable oil, e.g. sunflower,
   for frying
lemon wedges and tomato
   ketchup or vegan-friendly
   barbecue sauce, to serve

For the coating:
180ml/6fl oz (¾ cup)
   unsweetened almond milk
100g/3½oz (1 cup) plain
   (all-purpose) flour
1 tsp sweet paprika
good pinch of cayenne pepper
½ tsp salt
freshly ground black pepper
175g/6oz (2 cups) dried
   breadcrumbs

Who says jackfruit isn't versatile? These crispy fried bites taste delicious and are a great vegan substitute for chicken nuggets. Easy to prepare and quick to cook, they make a great snack, or you can serve them with French fries and salad or vegetables for supper.

1 Mix together the soy sauce, agave syrup and garlic powder. Brush over the jackfruit pieces (leave them whole – don't slice or shred) and set aside for 15 minutes.

2 To make the coating, put the almond milk in a bowl. Put the flour, spices, salt and pepper in another shallow bowl and mix together. Put the dried breadcrumbs in a third shallow bowl.

3 Dust the jackfruit pieces with the flour mixture and dip them quickly into the almond milk. Repeat this twice, then roll them lightly in the breadcrumbs.

4 Heat the oil for frying in a large frying pan (skillet) set over a medium to high heat and when it's hot add the nuggets, a few at a time. Fry for 6–8 minutes, turning them once or twice, until golden brown and crispy.

5 Serve immediately with lemon wedges and tomato ketchup or barbecue sauce.

OR YOU CAN TRY THIS...

– Brush the jackfruit pieces with mustard.
– If you're not vegan, use beaten egg instead of the almond milk.

BREAKFASTS, BRUNCHES & SALADS

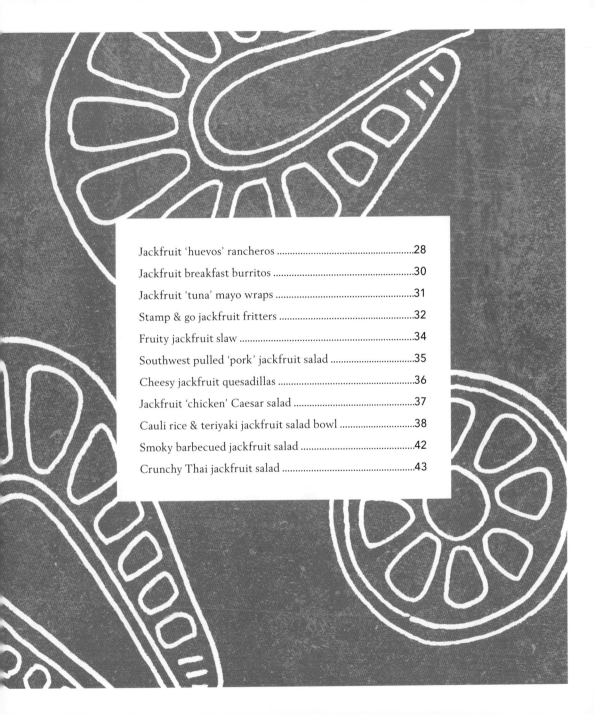

JACKFRUIT 'HUEVOS' RANCHEROS

SERVES: 4 | **PREP:** 15 MINUTES | **CHILL:** 30 MINUTES | **COOK:** 30 MINUTES

400g/14oz can green
   jackfruit in brine,
   drained and rinsed
4 tbsp olive oil
juice of 1 lime
1 tsp aminos (liquid smoke)
1 tsp chilli powder
1 tbsp brown sugar
1 large red onion, finely
   chopped
2 garlic cloves, crushed
1 hot red chilli, diced
2 red (bell) peppers,
   deseeded and diced
400g/14oz can chopped
   tomatoes
150ml/¼ pint (generous
   ½ cup) vegetable stock
   (broth)
4 large corn or flour tortillas
salt and freshly ground
   black pepper
a few sprigs of coriander
   (cilantro), chopped

For the scramble:
1 tbsp olive oil
400g/14oz extra-firm
   or firm tofu
¼ tsp salt
¼ tsp ground turmeric

Eat these vegan Mexican-style 'scrambled eggs' and jackfruit for a weekend breakfast or brunch. You can make the spicy tomato sauce in advance and reheat just before serving.

1 Slice the jackfruit and mix in a bowl with 1 tablespoon of the olive oil, the lime juice, aminos and chilli powder. Cover and marinate in the fridge for 30 minutes.

2 Heat 1 tablespoon of the oil in a frying pan (skillet) set over a medium heat and cook the jackfruit, stirring occasionally, for 8–10 minutes. Increase the heat, add the sugar and cook for 2–3 minutes until browned. Shred with 2 forks and keep warm.

3 Meanwhile, heat the remaining oil in another pan set over a medium heat and cook the onion, garlic, chilli and red peppers, stirring occasionally, for 8–10 minutes until tender. Lower the heat and add the tomatoes and stock. Cook for 6–8 minutes until reduced and thickened. Season with salt and pepper.

4 Make the scramble: heat the oil in a frying pan set over a medium to high heat. With your hands, crumble the tofu into small bite-sized pieces into the pan and stir in the salt, turmeric and some black pepper. Cook for 5–10 minutes, stirring occasionally and adding a little water to keep it moist if it gets too dry.

5 Warm the tortillas in a dry frying pan or a low oven and divide between 4 serving plates. Spread some hot tomato sauce over each one and top with the warm jackfruit and then the scramble mixture. Drizzle with more tomato sauce and sprinkle with chopped coriander. Serve immediately.

OR YOU CAN TRY THIS...
– Add some diced avocado and a squeeze of lime juice.
– Serve with a spoonful of vegan sour cream or coconut yoghurt.

JACKFRUIT BREAKFAST BURRITOS

SERVES: 4 | **PREP:** 15 MINUTES | **COOK:** 10 MINUTES

4 flour tortillas

8 heaped tbsp fresh hot tomato salsa

1 quantity jackfruit bacon (see page 15)

1 ripe avocado, peeled, stoned (pitted) and diced

85g/3oz (scant ½ cup) shredded vegan cheese

good pinch of crushed dried chilli flakes

a few sprigs of coriander (cilantro), chopped

4 tbsp coconut yoghurt or vegan sour cream

hot sauce, for drizzling

For the scramble:

1 tbsp olive oil

400g/14oz extra-firm or firm tofu

¼ tsp salt

¼ tsp ground turmeric

freshly ground black pepper

These spicy tofu scramble and jackfruit bacon burritos are quick and easy to make. Use Cheddar-style shredded cheese for its sharp flavour.

1 Heat the tortillas in a hot pan set over a low to medium heat for a few seconds. Remove and keep warm.

2 Make the scramble: heat the oil in a frying pan (skillet) set over a medium to high heat. With your hands, crumble the tofu into small bite-sized pieces into the pan and stir in the salt, turmeric and some black pepper. Cook for 5–10 minutes, stirring occasionally and adding a little water to keep it moist if it gets too dry.

3 Put a warm tortilla on each serving plate and spread with the tomato salsa. Add the scrambled tofu and crumble the crispy jackfruit bacon over the top. Add the avocado and sprinkle with the shredded cheese, chilli flakes and coriander. Top with the yoghurt or vegan sour cream.

4 Fold the sides of each tortilla over the filling then roll it up from the bottom. Serve immediately, drizzled with hot sauce.

OR YOU CAN TRY THIS...

– Add diced spring onions (scallions) to the scrambled tofu mixture.

– If you don't have jackfruit bacon, use some pulled jackfruit instead.

JACKFRUIT 'TUNA' MAYO WRAPS

SERVES: 4 | **PREP:** 15 MINUTES | **COOK:** 15-20 MINUTES

olive oil spray
½ small onion, finely
   chopped
1 garlic clove, crushed
400g/14oz can green
   jackfruit in brine,
   drained, rinsed and
   shredded
1 tsp kelp granules or
   seaweed dulse
200g/7oz (1 cup) canned
   cannellini beans, drained
   and mashed
4 tbsp mayonnaise
2 tsp Dijon mustard
juice of 1 small lemon
4 large slices Cheddar
   cheese
4 tortilla wraps
shredded salad leaves and
   sliced tomatoes, to serve

Canned jackfruit can be transformed into a fishy tuna-style substitute by shredding and cooking with kelp granules or seaweed dulse, which impart a taste of the sea. You can buy them online or from health and wholefood stores. To make this vegan, just use vegan mayonnaise and cheese.

1 Lightly spray a frying pan (skillet) with oil and set over a medium heat. Cook the onion and garlic for 4–5 minutes until tender. Add the shredded jackfruit and cook, stirring occasionally, for at least 5 minutes until the mixture is dry. Stir in the kelp granules or dulse.

2 Transfer the jackfruit to a bowl and mix with the mashed beans, mayonnaise, mustard and lemon juice.

3 Place a slice of cheese in the centre of each tortilla and pop under a hot grill (broiler) until the cheese melts.

4 Top with the 'tuna' mayo mixture, salad leaves and tomatoes. Fold the sides of each wrap in towards the centre to enclose the filling, then tuck in the ends. Pop them back under the grill for 2–3 minutes until lightly browned.

OR YOU CAN TRY THIS...

– Use 100g/3½oz (1 cup) grated cheese instead of sliced.
– Add some canned sweetcorn kernels to the tuna 'mayo' mixture.
– Serve in a toasted sandwich instead of wraps.
– Add a little nam pla (Thai fish sauce) to the jackfruit.
– Use dried seaweed (nori) flakes instead of kelp granules.

STAMP & GO JACKFRUIT FRITTERS

SERVES: 4 | **PREP:** 15 MINUTES | **COOK:** 15-20 MINUTES

400g/14oz can green
   jackfruit in brine,
   drained, rinsed and
   shredded
2 tbsp soy sauce
juice of 1 lime
1 tbsp seaweed (nori) flakes
1 small red (bell) pepper,
   deseeded and diced
6 spring onions (scallions),
   finely chopped
2 garlic cloves, crushed
1 Scotch bonnet chilli, diced
½ tsp smoked paprika
½ tsp sugar
1 tsp chopped thyme
a handful of coriander
   (cilantro), chopped
150g/5oz (2 cups) gram
   (chickpea) flour
2 tsp baking powder
100ml/3½fl oz (scant
   ½ cup) water
salt and freshly ground
   black pepper
vegetable oil, for frying
hot sauce, for drizzling

In the Caribbean, fish fritters – known locally as 'stamp and go' – are widely eaten for breakfast. Here's a vegan, gluten-free version using shredded jackfruit and chickpea flour.

1 Mix the shredded jackfruit, soy sauce, lime juice and seaweed flakes in a large bowl. Add the red pepper, spring onions, garlic, chilli, paprika, sugar and herbs. Stir well to distribute everything evenly and then mix in the gram flour, baking powder and seasoning.

2 Now stir in enough water to make the mixture stick together and form a thick batter. If it's too dry, add a little more water.

3 Heat the vegetable oil in a large frying pan (skillet) set over a medium to high heat – you want a depth of about 5mm/¼in. When the oil is really hot, add heaped tablespoons of the batter to the pan and fry in batches for 4–5 minutes on each side until crisp and golden brown. Remove and drain on kitchen paper (paper towels) and keep warm while you cook the remaining fritters in the same way.

4 Serve the fritters immediately, drizzled with hot sauce.

OR YOU CAN TRY THIS...
– Use kelp granules or seaweed dulse instead of nori.
– Serve with sliced or mashed avocado.
– Use plain (all-purpose) flour instead of chickpea flour.

FRUITY JACKFRUIT SLAW

SERVES: 4 | **PREP:** 15 MINUTES

200g/7oz red cabbage,
  shredded
200g/7oz white or green
  cabbage, shredded
1 large carrot, grated
1 fresh red chilli, deseeded
  and shredded
200g/7oz fresh ripe
  jackfruit, deseeded and
  cut into matchsticks
2 sweet apples, peeled,
  cored and cut into
  matchsticks
juice of 1 lime
1 tsp diced pickled ginger
a handful of coriander
  (cilantro), chopped
salt and freshly ground
  black pepper

For the vinaigrette dressing:
3 tbsp olive oil
1 tbsp cider vinegar
1 tbsp ginger pickling liquid
1 tbsp soft brown sugar

This healthy, tangy slaw uses sweet, ripe jackfruit. You can buy it fresh and pre-packed in many Asian food markets and delis, or use the canned variety packed in syrup (see Tip). The tropical flavour is reminiscent of pineapple, banana and mango. In this recipe, the sweetness is offset by the vinegar and pickled ginger.

1 Make the dressing: mix all the ingredients together in a bowl until well combined and the sugar has dissolved.

2 In a large bowl, mix together the shredded cabbage, carrot, chilli and jackfruit. Toss the apple matchsticks in the lime juice and add to the bowl with the pickled ginger and coriander. Season lightly with salt and pepper.

3 Toss gently in the dressing until everything is lightly coated.

OR YOU CAN TRY THIS...
– Add some shredded red onion, spring onions (scallions) or radishes to the slaw.
– Use chopped parsley or mint instead of coriander.
– Substitute grated fresh root ginger for the pickled ginger.

TIP: If you can't get fresh jackfruit, use canned in syrup and drain and discard the syrup.

SOUTHWEST PULLED 'PORK' JACKFRUIT SALAD

SERVES: 4 | **PREP:** 20 MINUTES | **COOK:** 15 MINUTES

400g/14oz can green jackfruit in brine, drained and rinsed
1 tbsp olive oil
2 tsp soft brown sugar
1 tsp smoked paprika
1 tsp chilli powder
½ tsp ground cumin
½ tsp dried thyme or oregano
¼ tsp garlic powder
¼ tsp onion powder
1 crisp cos (romaine) lettuce, sliced
¼ red onion, diced
1 courgette (zucchini), cut into matchsticks
4 ripe tomatoes, roughly chopped
a handful of flat-leaf parsley or coriander (cilantro), chopped

For the southwest dressing:
3 tbsp olive oil
1 tbsp cider vinegar
1 tbsp lime or lemon juice
1 garlic clove, crushed
1 ripe avocado, peeled, stoned (pitted) and mashed
salt and freshly ground black pepper

The chilli, spices and mashed avocado dressing give this salad a taste of the southwest of the United States. Eat it as a main course by serving it with tortillas, rice pilaf or roasted sweet potato chunks.

1 With your hands, squeeze out the water from the jackfruit pieces and pat dry with kitchen paper (paper towels). Discard the seeds and shred the jackfruit with your fingers or 2 forks.

2 Heat the oil in a frying pan (skillet) set over a medium to high heat. Cook the jackfruit, stirring occasionally, for 5 minutes, or until it starts to brown. Stir in the sugar, spices, herbs, garlic and onion powders and 100ml/3½fl oz (scant ½ cup) water. Cook for about 10 minutes, stirring occasionally, until the jackfruit is dry, browned and crispy.

3 Meanwhile, make the dressing: whisk the olive oil, vinegar, lime or lemon juice and garlic together in a jug or bowl. Stir in the mashed avocado and season to taste.

4 Put the lettuce, red onion, courgette and tomatoes into a large bowl. Toss gently in the dressing and scatter the chopped herbs over the top. Divide between 4 serving plates or bowls and top with the jackfruit.

OR YOU CAN TRY THIS...
– Add some chickpeas or red kidney beans to the salad.
– Add some spring onions (scallions), cucumber or carrot ribbons (made with a potato peeler).

CHEESY JACKFRUIT QUESADILLAS

SERVES: 4 | **PREP:** 15 MINUTES | **COOK:** 35 MINUTES

1 tbsp olive oil, plus extra
    for brushing
1 small onion, diced
2 garlic cloves, crushed
1 tsp chipotle or chilli
    powder
1 tsp ground cumin
1 fresh or pickled jalapeño
    chilli, diced
1 tsp demerara sugar
400g/14oz can green
    jackfruit in brine,
    drained, rinsed and sliced
100g/3½oz (1 cup) grated
    Cheddar cheese
a small bunch of coriander
    (cilantro), chopped
1 ripe avocado, peeled,
    stoned (pitted) and diced
juice of 1 lime
4 large flour tortillas
salt and freshly ground
    black pepper
chilli sauce, for drizzling

These spicy quesadillas are really quick and easy. You could make the pulled jackfruit in advance so you have everything prepared when you're ready to cook. For a vegan version, use shredded vegan Cheddar-style cheese.

1 Preheat the oven to 220°C, 425°F, gas mark 7. Line a baking tray (cookie sheet) with baking parchment.

2 Heat the oil in a frying pan (skillet) set over a medium heat and cook the onion and garlic for 5 minutes until tender. Stir in the spices, jalapeño chilli and sugar and cook for 2 minutes. Add the jackfruit and cook for a further 5 minutes. Shred with a fork and season to taste.

3 Tip the jackfruit mixture onto the lined baking tray, spreading it out, and bake in the oven for at least 10 minutes, or until well browned and dry.

4 In a bowl, mix together the cheese, coriander, avocado and lime juice. Divide the mixture between 2 of the tortillas, leaving a thin border around the edges. Top with the jackfruit and place the other 2 tortillas on top. Press firmly together around the edges.

5 Brush a large non-stick frying pan with oil and set over a medium to high heat. When it's really hot, place a quesadilla in the pan and cook for 3 minutes, or until crisp and golden underneath. Flip it over carefully and cook the other side. The filling should be hot and the cheese melting. Slide the quesadilla out of the pan and keep warm while you cook the other one in the same way.

6 Cut each quesadilla into 4 wedges. Eat immediately, drizzled with chilli sauce.

OR YOU CAN TRY THIS...
– Add some refried beans or smashed red kidney beans.
– Serve with sour cream, yoghurt, guacamole or fresh salsa.

JACKFRUIT 'CHICKEN' CAESAR SALAD

SERVES: 4 | **PREP:** 15 MINUTES | **COOK:** 15 MINUTES

4 thick slices day-old bread
2 garlic cloves, crushed
1 tbsp olive oil, plus extra
for drizzling
2 x 400g/14oz cans green
jackfruit in brine, drained
and rinsed
½ tsp smoked paprika
2 heads cos (romaine)
lettuce, roughly torn
12 baby plum tomatoes,
halved
4 tbsp grated Parmesan
cheese, plus extra for
sprinkling

For the Caesar dressing:
1 large garlic clove, crushed
1 medium free-range
egg yolk
grated zest and juice of
1 lemon
a few drops of
Worcestershire sauce
1 tsp Dijon mustard
120ml/4fl oz (½ cup)
extra-virgin olive oil

This vegetarian Caesar salad uses jackfruit instead of chicken. Vegans can make a Caesar dressing by blending some vegan mayo with garlic, lemon juice and Dijon mustard, and can substitute shredded vegan cheese for the Parmesan.

1 Preheat the oven to 200°C, 400°F, gas mark 6.

2 Cut the bread into small cubes and place in a bowl with the garlic. Drizzle with olive oil and stir gently. Place on a baking tray (cookie sheet) and bake in the oven for 15 minutes, or until crisp and golden brown all over.

3 Meanwhile, with your hands, squeeze out the water from the jackfruit pieces and pat dry with kitchen paper (paper towels). Discard the seeds and the hard cores. Heat the oil in a frying pan (skillet) over a medium to high heat. Add the jackfruit pieces and smoked paprika and cook for 10–15 minutes, stirring occasionally.

4 Make the dressing: blitz the garlic, egg yolk, lemon zest and juice, Worcestershire sauce and mustard in a blender. Add the olive oil in a thin stream through the feed tube until you have a fairly thick, creamy dressing. Taste it and add more lemon juice or some cider or white wine vinegar if you like it more piquant.

5 Put the lettuce, tomatoes and jackfruit in a serving bowl and toss gently in the dressing. Add the Parmesan and toss again. Sprinkle with the bread croutons and more Parmesan and serve.

OR YOU CAN TRY THIS...
– Add some grated Parmesan to the dressing.
– Add some spring onions (scallions) and chopped parsley or dill to the salad.
– Slice or shred the jackfruit and add 'raw' to the lettuce and tomatoes.

CAULI RICE & TERIYAKI JACKFRUIT SALAD BOWL

SERVES: 4 | **PREP:** 20 MINUTES | **COOK:** 20 MINUTES

1 tsp sesame oil
2 tbsp dark soy sauce
2 tbsp mirin
2 tbsp rice wine vinegar
2 tbsp soft brown sugar
1 tsp diced fresh root ginger
2 x 400g/14oz cans green
   jackfruit in brine, drained
   and rinsed
2 tbsp white sesame seeds

For the cauliflower rice:
1 small cauliflower
2 tbsp groundnut
   (peanut) oil
2 lemongrass stalks,
   peeled and diced
1 red chilli, diced
a bunch of spring onions
   (scallions), thinly sliced
75g/3oz (generous 1 cup)
   grated carrot
75g/3oz (generous
   1 cup) grated courgette
   (zucchini)
3 kaffir lime leaves,
   shredded
a bunch of mint,
   finely chopped
a bunch of coriander
   (cilantro), finely chopped

This low-carb cauliflower 'rice' salad is full of citrus, spicy, salty and sweet flavours. You can make it in advance and keep it overnight in the fridge until you're ready to cook the jackfruit. Vegans can substitute soy sauce or vegan fish sauce for the nam pla in the dressing.

1 Make the cauliflower rice: cut the leaves and stem from the cauliflower and pulse the florets in a food processor until they have the consistency of rice-sized 'grains'.

2 Heat the groundnut oil in a wok or deep frying pan (skillet) set over a medium to high heat. Stir-fry the lemongrass, chilli and spring onions for 2–3 minutes. Add the cauliflower rice and stir-fry for 4–5 minutes until tender but still slightly crunchy.

3 Transfer to a large bowl and mix with the grated carrot and courgette, lime leaves and herbs.

4 Make the citrus dressing: blend all the ingredients together, then sprinkle over the warm cauliflower and toss gently. Cover and chill in the fridge while you cook the jackfruit.

5 Mix the sesame oil, soy sauce, mirin, vinegar and sugar in a bowl to make a teriyaki glaze. Dry the jackfruit pieces with kitchen paper (paper towels) and shred with 2 forks.

For the citrus dressing:
juice of 2 limes
2 tbsp nam pla
(Thai fish sauce)
1 tbsp caster (superfine)
sugar

6 Heat a non-stick frying pan (skillet) set over a medium to high heat and add the jackfruit. Cook for 4–5 minutes, stirring and tossing, until dry and starting to colour. Stir in the sesame oil mixture and cook gently until it reduces and the jackfruit is glazed and glossy.

7 Divide the cauli rice between 4 serving bowls and add the jackfruit. Sprinkle with the sesame seeds and serve.

OR YOU CAN TRY THIS...
– Use a ready-made teriyaki sauce.
– Sprinkle with toasted sesame seeds.

SMOKY BARBECUED JACKFRUIT SALAD

SERVES: 4 | **PREP:** 15 MINUTES | **COOK:** 12-18 MINUTES

2 x 400g/14oz cans green jackfruit in brine, drained and rinsed

1 tsp olive oil

2 medium avocados, peeled, stoned (pitted) and sliced

juice of ½ lemon or lime

300g/10½ oz cherry tomatoes

a few handfuls of salad leaves, e.g. crisp lettuce, radicchio, chicory, rocket (arugula), shredded kale or spinach

vinaigrette dressing, for drizzling

For the barbecue sauce:
240ml/8fl oz (1 cup) tomato ketchup

2 tbsp apple cider or red wine vinegar

2 tbsp vegan Worcestershire sauce (see Tip)

3 tbsp soft brown sugar

1 tbsp vegan Dijon mustard

1 tsp smoked paprika

1 tsp chilli powder

salt and freshly ground black pepper

Adding smoked paprika to the barbecue sauce gives the pulled jackfruit a subtle smoky flavour in this colourful salad. The great thing about salad bowls is that you can add almost anything, including leftovers, to make them more of a main meal.

1 With your hands, squeeze out the water from the jackfruit pieces and pat dry with kitchen paper (paper towels). Discard the seeds and cut the jackfruit into slices.

2 Mix together all the ingredients for the barbecue sauce in a bowl.

3 Heat the oil in a frying pan (skillet) set over a medium heat. Add the jackfruit and cook for 2–3 minutes. Pour in the barbecue sauce and stir well to coat the jackfruit. Cook for 10–15 minutes until the mixture is glossy and the sauce has reduced, then shred the jackfruit with 2 forks.

4 Divide the jackfruit between 4 shallow bowls. Toss the avocado slices in the lemon or lime juice and add to the bowls together with the tomatoes and salad leaves. Drizzle with some vinaigrette and eat immediately while the jackfruit is still hot.

OR YOU CAN TRY THIS...

– Make the salad bowl more substantial by adding some cooked brown rice or quinoa, rice noodles or pasta, lentils, canned beans, falafels or chickpeas.

TIP: You can buy vegan Worcestershire sauce (the regular sort contains anchovies) online and in some supermarkets and health food stores. Or you can substitute some soy sauce or tamari.

CRUNCHY THAI JACKFRUIT SALAD

SERVES: 4 | **PREP:** 20 MINUTES

400g/14oz can green
jackfruit in brine,
drained and rinsed
200g/7oz beansprouts
2 carrots, peeled and cut
into matchsticks
2 red (bell) peppers,
deseeded and thinly
sliced
6 spring onions (scallions),
sliced
8 crisp radishes, thinly
sliced
½ cucumber, cut into thin
matchsticks
a handful of coriander
(cilantro), chopped
1 red bird's-eye chilli, cut
into thin shreds
30g/1oz (¼ cup) roasted
peanuts, chopped
1 tbsp toasted sesame seeds
salt and freshly ground
black pepper

For the dressing:
1 tbsp groundnut (peanut) oil
1 tsp toasted sesame oil
2 tbsp nam pla (Thai fish
sauce)
1 tbsp rice vinegar
juice of 1 lime
1 garlic clove, crushed
1 tbsp sugar

This zingy salad is very refreshing and great in winter when salad leaves and tomatoes are not in season. Vegetarians and vegans can use soy sauce, tamari or vegan 'fish' sauce instead of nam pla in the dressing. Add some stir-fried tofu and rice noodles to transform the salad into a main course.

1 Make the dressing: put all the ingredients in a bowl and whisk together until thoroughly combined and the sugar has dissolved.

2 Use your hands to gently squeeze out any water from the jackfruit pieces and pat dry with kitchen paper (paper towels). Cut off the firm parts at the apex of each triangle and remove the seeds. Slice the jackfruit thinly.

3 In a bowl, mix together the beansprouts, carrots, red peppers, spring onions, radishes, cucumber and most of the coriander. Gently stir in the jackfruit.

4 Toss lightly in the dressing and season to taste with salt and pepper. Sprinkle with the remaining coriander, and the chilli, peanuts and sesame seeds.

OR YOU CAN TRY THIS...
– Add some edamame (soy) beans or blanched fine green beans.
– Drizzle the salad with sweet chilli sauce.
– Add some crunchy peanut butter to the dressing.
– Add some stir-fried sliced 'meaty' mushrooms.

LIGHT MEALS

RICE & JACKFRUIT STUFFED SQUASH

SERVES: 4 | **PREP:** 20 MINUTES | **COOK:** 40 MINUTES

4 medium butternut or
    acorn squash, halved
    and deseeded
4 tbsp olive oil, plus extra
    for brushing
2 tbsp maple syrup
1 red onion, diced
2 garlic cloves, crushed
1 tsp cumin seeds
1 tsp smoked paprika
1 tsp chilli powder
1 red (bell) pepper,
    deseeded and diced
1 tbsp tomato purée (paste)
400g/14oz can green
    jackfruit, drained,
    rinsed and sliced
2 ripe tomatoes, diced
150g/5½oz baby spinach
250g/9oz (1 cup) cooked
    brown rice
a few sprigs of flat-leaf
    parsley, chopped
salt and freshly ground
    black pepper

Tender squash with a nutty brown rice and spicy jackfruit stuffing makes a great lunch or light supper. Serve it hot with some green vegetables or at room temperature with a crisp salad.

1 Preheat the oven to 200°C, 400°F, gas mark 6.

2 With a sharp knife, score a diagonal pattern in the flesh of each squash half. Lightly brush with 2 tablespoons of the olive oil and the maple syrup. Place on a baking tray (cookie sheet) and bake in the oven for about 40 minutes, or until tender.

3 Meanwhile, heat the remaining oil in a large frying pan (skillet) set over a medium heat. Cook the onion and garlic, stirring occasionally, for 6–8 minutes. Stir in the cumin seeds, spices and red pepper and cook for 5 minutes.

4 Stir in the tomato purée, then add the jackfruit and tomatoes. Cook for 10 minutes, then shred the jackfruit with 2 forks. Add the spinach and cook for 2–3 minutes until it wilts. Stir in the rice and most of the parsley.

5 Scoop out the flesh in the centre of the cooked squash halves, leaving a thin border around the outside. Dice the flesh and add to the jackfruit and rice mixture. Cook for 2–3 minutes until everything is warmed through and season with salt and pepper.

6 Divide the mixture between the hollowed-out squash halves and serve immediately, sprinkled with the rest of the parsley.

OR YOU CAN TRY THIS...
– Stir in some chopped pecans or walnuts.
– Use cooked quinoa instead of rice.
– Use the mixture to stuff baked peppers, beef tomatoes or aubergines (eggplants).

JACKFRUIT STUFFED AVOCADOS

SERVES: 4 | **PREP:** 15 MINUTES | **COOK:** 20-30 MINUTES

400g/14oz can green jackfruit, drained and rinsed

1 tsp olive oil, plus extra for drizzling

1 garlic clove, crushed

½ tsp ground cumin

½ tsp paprika

¼ tsp dried oregano

1 tsp tomato purée (paste)

1 tsp soy sauce

1 tsp soft dark brown sugar

4 ripe medium-sized avocados

75g/3oz sun-blush tomatoes, drained and chopped

50g/2oz (½ cup) toasted pine nuts

a handful of flat-leaf parsley, chopped

1–2 tbsp green pesto

4 tbsp fresh breadcrumbs

2 tbsp grated Parmesan cheese

salt and freshly ground black pepper

hot sauce, e.g. Sriracha, for drizzling

If you've never thought of stuffing and baking avocados, now's the time to try. You'll be surprised at how good they are. To make a vegan version, just use grated vegan cheese and vegan pesto.

1 Preheat the oven to 200°C, 400°F, gas mark 6.

2 Squeeze any liquid out of the jackfruit pieces and pat dry with kitchen paper (paper towels). Shred them with 2 forks or use your hands to pull them apart.

3 Heat the oil in a non-stick frying pan (skillet) set over a medium heat and add the jackfruit, garlic, spices, tomato purée, soy sauce and sugar. Cook, stirring occasionally, for 10–15 minutes until browned and crisp.

4 Meanwhile, cut the avocados in half lengthways and discard the stones (pits). Hollow them out with a teaspoon and mix the scooped-out flesh in a bowl with the sun-blush tomatoes, pine nuts, parsley and pesto. Add the jackfruit and season lightly with salt and pepper.

5 Use this mixture to fill the avocado halves and place them in a large roasting pan – they should fit snugly so they can't topple over during cooking. Sprinkle with the breadcrumbs and Parmesan and drizzle a little olive oil over the top.

6 Bake in the oven for 10–15 minutes until crisp and golden brown. Drizzle with hot sauce and serve immediately with a crisp salad.

OR YOU CAN TRY THIS...

– Fill the avocado halves with salsa, top with the breadcrumbs and Parmesan and bake as above.

– Use chopped walnuts instead of pine nuts.

– Swap the sun-blush tomatoes for diced cherry or baby plum tomatoes.

VIETNAMESE JACKFRUIT BANH MI

SERVES: 4 | **PREP:** 20 MINUTES | **STAND:** AT LEAST 1 HOUR | **COOK:** 20 MINUTES

2 carrots, cut into thin matchsticks
4 radishes, thinly sliced
1 red (bell) pepper, deseeded and thinly sliced
1 small cucumber, thinly sliced
4 tbsp rice vinegar
4 tbsp caster (superfine) sugar
1 tbsp nam pla (Thai fish sauce)
4 small baguettes (French sticks), halved and hollowed out
120g/4oz (½ cup) mayonnaise
2 tbsp Sriracha or Thai sweet chilli sauce
1 red onion, thinly sliced

For the spicy jackfruit:
2 x 400g/14oz cans green jackfruit in brine, drained and rinsed
2 tbsp olive oil
1 small onion, diced
3 garlic cloves, crushed
2.5cm/1in piece fresh root ginger, diced
1 red bird's-eye chilli, diced
2 tbsp soy sauce or tamari
1 tsp tomato purée (paste)
2 tbsp soft brown sugar
a handful of coriander (cilantro), chopped

This takes longer to make than most sandwiches, but it's well worth the effort. We've substituted jackfruit for the traditional minced beef and it's delicious! For a veggie or vegan version, use vegan 'fish' sauce or some soy sauce or tamari in place of the nam pla.

1 Mix together the carrots, radishes, red pepper and cucumber in a glass bowl. Heat the vinegar and caster sugar in a small saucepan set over a medium heat, stirring until the sugar dissolves, then bring to the boil and remove from the heat. Stir in the nam pla and pour over the vegetables. Set aside for at least 1 hour – the longer the better.

2 Meanwhile, press as much water out of the jackfruit as possible and pat dry with kitchen paper (paper towels). Cut off and discard the tough tips on the triangles.

3 Heat the oil in a frying pan (skillet) set over a medium to high heat. Add the onion, garlic, ginger and chilli and cook, stirring occasionally, for 6–8 minutes until softened and golden. Reduce the heat to medium and stir in the jackfruit, soy sauce or tamari, tomato purée and brown sugar. Cook for at least 10 minutes until the jackfruit is brown and fragrant. Use 2 forks to shred it coarsely and stir in the coriander.

4 Split the baguettes in half lengthways and scoop out some of the soft bread in the centre to leave a crusty shell. Mix the mayonnaise with the hot sauce and spread over the baguette bases. Add the spicy jackfruit mixture and top with the carrot and radish mixture and the sliced onion. Cover with the baguette tops, pressing down firmly, and eat immediately.

OR YOU CAN TRY THIS...
– Add some pickled chillies to the baguette.
– Try chopped Thai basil or mint instead of coriander.
– Add some sliced spring onions (scallions) or crisp lettuce.

SPICY JACKFRUIT 'FISHCAKES'

SERVES: 4 | **PREP:** 15 MINUTES | **COOK:** 30 MINUTES

450g/1lb potatoes, peeled and cut into chunks
400g/14oz can green jackfruit, drained and rinsed
4 tbsp vegan mayonnaise
4 spring onions (scallions), finely chopped
2 garlic cloves, crushed
1 bird's-eye red chilli, deseeded and diced
2 kaffir lime leaves, finely chopped
a handful of coriander (cilantro), finely chopped
plain (all-purpose) flour, for dusting
4 tbsp vegetable oil, for frying
salt and freshly ground black pepper
sweet chilli sauce, for drizzling
lime wedges, for squeezing

You can prepare these fishcakes a few hours in advance and keep them chilled in the fridge, ready for frying. Serve them with salad or some rice noodles tossed in chilli oil or cooked in coconut milk.

1 Cook the potatoes in a large saucepan of salted boiling water for 15 minutes, or until tender but not mushy. Drain well, then return to the pan and mash with a fork or potato masher until smooth and lump free. Set aside to cool.

2 Press as much water out of the jackfruit as possible and pat dry with kitchen paper (paper towels). Cut off and discard the tough tips to the triangles and shred the jackfruit with 2 forks or your fingers.

3 Add to the cooled mashed potato with the mayonnaise, spring onions, garlic, chilli, lime leaves and coriander. Season with salt and pepper and mix well to distribute everything evenly throughout the potato mixture.

4 Take large spoonfuls of the mixture and, using your hands, shape them into patties, about 7.5cm/3in wide. Dust with flour, shaking off the excess.

5 Heat the oil in a large frying pan (skillet) set over a medium to high heat. When it's hot, add the fishcakes, a few at a time, and fry for about 3–4 minutes on each side until crisp and golden brown. Remove and drain on kitchen paper and keep warm while you cook the remainder in the same way.

6 Serve the hot fishcakes with sweet chilli sauce and some lime wedges for squeezing.

OR YOU CAN TRY THIS...

– If you're not vegan or vegetarian, add 1 tablespoon nam pla (Thai fish sauce) to the fishcake mixture.
– To make the cakes more 'fishy', you can add ½ teaspoon kelp granules or seaweed dulse.

JACKFRUIT GRILLED CHEESE SANDWICH

SERVES: 4 | **PREP:** 10 MINUTES | **COOK:** 18 MINUTES

400g/14oz can green
   jackfruit in brine,
   drained and rinsed
2 tsp olive oil or coconut oil
½ tsp smoked paprika
½ tsp garlic powder
¼ tsp dried oregano
4 tbsp hot sauce or
   barbecue sauce
1 tsp maple syrup
8 slices wholegrain or
   multi-seed bread
4 tbsp mayonnaise
4 slices mozzarella
1 sliced tomato or 4 thin
   slices red onion

Pulled barbecued jackfruit is a great filling for a toasted cheese sandwich. It doesn't take long to cook and has the texture and flavour of pulled pork. Vegans can use vegan mayo and sliced or shredded vegan mozzarella, or any vegan cheese of their choice.

1 Squeeze as much water out of the jackfruit as possible and pat dry with kitchen paper (paper towels). Cut each piece into 2 or 3 slices.

2 Heat the oil in a frying pan (skillet) set over a medium to high heat. Add the jackfruit, paprika, garlic powder and oregano and cook, stirring occasionally, for about 5 minutes, or until starting to brown. Shred the jackfruit with 2 forks and stir in the hot sauce or barbecue sauce and maple syrup. Cook for 10 minutes over a medium heat, or until the jackfruit is glossy and starting to crisp up.

3 Lightly toast the bread under a hot grill (broiler). Spread 4 slices with mayonnaise and cover with the jackfruit. Place a slice of mozzarella on top and pop back under the grill for 2–3 minutes until melted.

4 Arrange some sliced tomato or red onion on top and cover with the remaining toasted bread slices. Cut in half or into quarters and enjoy.

OR YOU CAN TRY THIS...
– Add some refried beans to the jackfruit.
– Add some jarred or roasted red and yellow (bell) peppers.
– Stir some baby spinach leaves into the jackfruit at the end of cooking.
– Use sourdough or ciabatta bread.

JACKFRUIT TACOS WITH SWEETCORN SALSA

SERVES: 4 | **PREP:** 15 MINUTES | **COOK:** 25-30 MINUTES

2 x 400g/14oz cans green
    jackfruit in brine, drained
    and rinsed
1 tbsp olive oil
1 red onion, chopped
4 garlic cloves, crushed
1 chipotle pepper, chopped
1 tsp ground cumin
½ tsp dried oregano
1–2 tbsp adobo sauce
1 tbsp tomato purée (paste)
8 soft flour tortillas
shredded crisp lettuce,
    e.g. cos (romaine)
soya or coconut yoghurt,
    to serve
1 lime, cut into wedges

For the sweetcorn salsa:
2 pieces of corn on the cob
olive oil, for brushing
½ red onion, diced
2 ripe avocados, peeled,
    stoned (pitted) and diced
juice of 2 limes
a handful of coriander
    (cilantro), chopped
good pinch of crushed
    chilli flakes
sea salt crystals

Pulled jackfruit makes the perfect filling for these delicious tacos. We've served them with a charred sweetcorn and avocado salsa, but if you're in a hurry, just roll up with some ready-made tomato salsa or guacamole. You can buy canned chipotle peppers in adobo sauce online or in many delis and specialist grocery stores.

1 Make the sweetcorn salsa: brush the corn cobs with oil and cook on a hot griddle (grill) pan or a barbecue, turning occasionally, for 10–12 minutes until tender and starting to char. Leave to cool, then remove the corn kernels with a sharp knife. Mix in a bowl with the onion, avocados, lime juice, coriander and chilli flakes. Season with salt, then cover and leave in the fridge.

2 Press as much water out of the jackfruit as possible and pat dry with kitchen paper (paper towels). Shred the jackfruit with 2 forks or your fingers.

3 Heat the oil in a non-stick frying pan (skillet) set over a medium heat and cook the onion and garlic, stirring occasionally, for 6–8 minutes, or until tender. Stir in the chipotle pepper, cumin and oregano and cook for 1 minute. Add the jackfruit and the adobo sauce and tomato purée. Cook for about 10 minutes until the sauce is reduced and fragrant and is coating the jackfruit.

4 Meanwhile, warm the tortillas in a dry frying pan set over a medium heat for 1–2 minutes each side.

5 Put some lettuce on each warm tortilla and top with the jackfruit mixture, sweetcorn salsa and yoghurt. Fold over or roll up and serve with lime wedges for squeezing.

OR YOU CAN TRY THIS...
– Add some canned black beans or refried beans to the tortillas.

CURRIED JACKFRUIT NAAN WRAPS

SERVES: 4 | **PREP:** 15 MINUTES | **COOK:** 20-25 MINUTES

4 vegan naan flatbreads
a few iceberg lettuce leaves, thinly sliced
½ small red onion, thinly sliced
4 tbsp coconut or soya yoghurt
4 tbsp mango chutney, to serve

For the curried jackfruit filling:
2 tbsp sunflower oil
1 onion, finely chopped
2 garlic cloves, crushed
2 sweet potatoes, peeled and diced
400g/14oz can green jackfruit, drained, rinsed and shredded
1 tbsp curry paste
1 tsp ground cumin
¼ tsp ground allspice
120ml/4fl oz (½ cup) canned coconut milk
100g/3½oz baby spinach leaves
salt and freshly ground black pepper

Soft naan flatbreads are delicious wrapped around a West Indian curried jackfruit and sweet potato filling. To make them more substantial, stir in some canned black beans or red kidney beans. Delicious!

1 Make the filling: heat the oil in a heavy-based frying pan (skillet) and cook the onion and garlic over a low to medium heat, stirring occasionally, for 5 minutes, or until softened. Add the sweet potatoes and jackfruit and cook for 5 minutes, stirring occasionally. Stir in the curry paste and ground spices.

2 Add the coconut milk and simmer gently for about 10–15 minutes, or until the vegetables are tender and the liquid has evaporated. A couple of minutes before the end of the cooking time, stir in the spinach and season to taste.

3 Preheat the oven to 200°C, 400°F, gas mark 6. Wrap the naan flatbreads in foil and heat in the oven for about 5 minutes.

4 Put some shredded lettuce on each warm naan flatbread and cover with the jackfruit filling. Top with the red onion, yoghurt and mango chutney. Fold the naan over the top and serve immediately.

OR YOU CAN TRY THIS...
– Use pumpkin or butternut squash instead of sweet potato.
– If you're not vegan, top with Greek yoghurt or cucumber raita.
– Instead of naan, use warm pitta bread or tortilla wraps.

JAMAICAN JERK JACKFRUIT BOWL

SERVES: 4 | **PREP:** 15 MINUTES | **COOK:** 20 MINUTES

2 x 400g/14oz cans green jackfruit in brine, drained and rinsed
1 tbsp coconut oil
4 spring onions (scallions)
175g/6oz (¾ cup) uncooked basmati rice
200ml/7fl oz (scant 1 cup) canned coconut milk
200ml/7fl oz (scant 1 cup) water
good pinch of salt
400g/14oz can red kidney beans, rinsed and drained
250g/9oz jarred roasted red (bell) peppers
2 medium avocados, peeled, stoned (pitted) and sliced
a handful of coriander (cilantro), chopped

For the jerk seasoning:
2 tsp allspice berries
2 tsp black peppercorns
1 tsp ground cinnamon
½ tsp dried thyme
1 shallot, diced
2 garlic cloves, crushed
2.5cm/1in piece fresh root ginger, chopped
2 Scotch bonnet chillies, deseeded and chopped
2 tbsp coconut sugar
2 tbsp soy sauce
juice of 1 lime

These colourful bowls have just the right balance of sweetness, heat and spice. Jerked food is often served in Jamaica with rice 'n' peas (the peas are actually kidney beans). We've cooked ours in coconut milk to give it a creamy, nutty flavour.

1 Make the jerk seasoning: pound the allspice berries in a pestle and mortar and then blitz with the all the other ingredients in a blender. Chop the spring onions.

2 Squeeze as much water out of the jackfruit as possible and pat dry with kitchen paper (paper towels). Tear each piece into thick shreds.

3 Heat the coconut oil in a large frying pan (skillet) set over a medium heat and cook the spring onions for 2–3 minutes. Add the jerk seasoning paste and cook, stirring, for 1 minute. Stir in the jackfruit and reduce the heat. Cook for 10–15 minutes until fragrant and tender.

4 Meanwhile, put the rice in a saucepan and cover with the coconut milk and water. Add the salt and bring to the boil. Reduce the heat to low and simmer gently, covered, for 12–15 minutes until all the liquid has been absorbed and the rice is cooked and tender. Set aside for 10 minutes, then fluff up with a fork and stir in the kidney beans.

5 Divide the rice between 4 shallow serving bowls. Add the jerked jackfruit, the peppers and avocados and sprinkle with coriander. Serve warm.

OR YOU CAN TRY THIS...
– Serve with some mango chutney or pineapple salsa.
– Add spring onions, fresh pineapple or toasted cashews to the cooked rice.
– Serve Jamaican-style with fried plantains.
– Squeeze some lime juice over the top.

JACKFRUIT GYROS WITH TZATZIKI

SERVES: 4 | **PREP:** 20 MINUTES | **COOK:** 30 MINUTES

2 x 400g/14oz cans green
   jackfruit in brine, drained
   and rinsed
2 tbsp olive oil, plus extra
   for brushing
1 red onion, finely chopped
3 garlic cloves, crushed
½ tsp ground cumin
½ tsp sweet paprika
1 tsp dried oregano
1 tbsp tomato purée (paste)
3 tbsp soy sauce
2 tbsp soft brown sugar
2 aubergines (eggplants),
   thickly sliced
1 tsp za'atar
4 large, thick pitta flatbreads
¼ cucumber, sliced
4 tomatoes, quartered
crisp lettuce leaves, shredded
salt and freshly ground
   black pepper

Gyros are Greek street food, traditionally made with meat or chicken, then wrapped up with salad and fried potatoes in a thick, soft flatbread and drizzled with garlic sauce. But you can make this wonderful vegan version with jackfruit and aubergines (eggplants).

1 Make the tzatziki: mix all the ingredients together in a bowl. Season to taste with salt and pepper.

2 Squeeze as much water out of the jackfruit as possible and pat dry with kitchen paper (paper towels).

3 Heat the oil in a large frying pan (skillet) set over a medium heat and cook the red onion and garlic, stirring occasionally, for 8–10 minutes until tender and golden. Stir in the spices, oregano and tomato purée and cook for 1 minute. Add the jackfruit, soy sauce and sugar and cook gently for 15 minutes. Flake the jackfruit with 2 forks.

4 Meanwhile, brush the aubergine slices on both sides with oil. Sprinkle with the za'atar and season with salt and pepper. Cook in batches on a large ridged griddle (grill) pan set over a medium to high heat for 2–3 minutes each side, or until charred, golden brown and striped. Drain on kitchen paper and keep warm.

5 Assemble the gyros: warm the flatbreads in a low oven or on a lightly oiled griddle pan. Divide the aubergines, jackfruit, cucumber, tomatoes and lettuce between them. Season lightly with salt and pepper and drizzle with the tzatziki. Fold up or roll over each flatbread to enclose the filling. Eat immediately.

For the tzatziki:
240ml/8fl oz (1 cup)
    coconut or soya yoghurt
1 tbsp olive oil
½ cucumber, diced
2 garlic cloves, crushed
a few sprigs of mint, finely
    chopped
a few sprigs of dill, finely
    chopped
grated zest and juice of
    ½ lemon

OR YOU CAN TRY THIS...

– Use hummus or tahini sauce instead of tzatziki.
– Drizzle with hot chilli sauce or harissa.
– Squeeze some fresh lemon juice over the gyros.
– Top with some thinly sliced red onion.

JACKFRUIT & SWEETCORN BUDDHA BOWL

SERVES: 4 | **PREP:** 15 MINUTES | **COOK:** 35 MINUTES

5 tbsp olive oil

2 onions, diced

3 garlic cloves, crushed

1 tsp cumin seeds

1 tsp crushed coriander seeds

400g/14oz can chopped
   tomatoes

2 tbsp tomato purée (paste)

1 tbsp brown sugar

2 x 400g/14oz cans green
   jackfruit in brine, drained
   and rinsed

120ml/4fl oz (½ cup)
   vegetable stock (broth)
   or water

a handful of flat-leaf parsley,
   finely chopped

400g/14oz canned sweetcorn
   kernels, drained

1 red chilli, diced

juice of 1 lime

2 ripe medium avocados,
   peeled, stoned (pitted)
   and sliced

salt and freshly ground
   black pepper

hot sauce or harissa,
   for drizzling

Don't be put off by the long list of ingredients. These aromatic bowls are really easy to prepare, cook and assemble. They are very versatile and you can experiment with different ingredients and flavourings depending on what you've got in your fridge or kitchen cupboards.

1 Rinse the quinoa under cold running water and drain in a sieve. Put the stock in a saucepan set over a low heat. Tip the quinoa into the stock, cover and simmer gently for 15 minutes, or until the quinoa is tender and has absorbed most of the stock – you'll know it's cooked when the sprout pops out of each seed. Let stand for 5 minutes before straining off any excess stock. Fluff up with a fork and stir in the chickpeas. Season with salt and pepper and keep warm.

2 Meanwhile, heat 3 tablespoons of the oil in a large frying pan (skillet) set over a medium heat. Cook the onions, garlic and spices for 8–10 minutes until fragrant and the onions are tender. Add the tomatoes, tomato purée and sugar and cook for 10 minutes until the mixture reduces and thickens.

3 Stir in the jackfruit and stock or water and bring to the boil. Reduce the heat and simmer gently for 12–15 minutes until everything is tender. Shred the jackfruit with 2 forks and stir in the parsley.

LIGHT MEALS

For the quinoa and chickpeas:
200g/7oz (scant 1¼ cups)
    uncooked quinoa
480ml/16fl oz (2 cups)
    boiling vegetable stock
400g/14oz can chickpeas,
    rinsed and drained

4 While the jackfruit is cooking, heat the remaining oil in a frying pan over a medium to high heat and stir-fry the sweetcorn, stirring occasionally, for 6–8 minutes until it starts to colour. Stir in the chilli and season to taste. Add a spoonful of lime juice.

5 Divide the quinoa and chickpeas between 4 shallow bowls and top with the jackfruit mixture. Add the corn kernels to each bowl together with the sliced avocados tossed in the rest of the lime juice. Drizzle with hot sauce or harissa and serve warm.

OR YOU CAN TRY THIS...
– Toss the quinoa and chickpeas in a lemony vinaigrette.
– Add some roasted vegetables, e.g. (bell) peppers and
  aubergine (eggplant).
– Sprinkle with chopped herbs, e.g. coriander (cilantro) or parsley.
– Drizzle with yoghurt or tahini.

JACKFRUIT & LEMONY PESTO COURGETTI

SERVES: 4 | **PREP:** 15 MINUTES | **COOK:** 20 MINUTES

400g/14oz can green
   jackfruit in brine, drained
   and rinsed
3 tbsp olive oil
1 onion, diced
4 garlic cloves, crushed
1 tbsp maple syrup
90ml/3fl oz (scant ½ cup)
   vegetable stock (broth)
1 tsp smoked paprika
4 large courgettes (zucchini)
120ml/4fl oz (½ cup)
   white wine
grated zest and juice of
   1 lemon
a handful of flat-leaf parsley,
   chopped
4 tbsp fresh green pesto
300g/10oz baby plum
   tomatoes, halved
salt and freshly ground
   black pepper
grated Parmesan cheese,
   for sprinkling

Courgette (zucchini) ribbons are the perfect low-carb and gluten-free substitute for pasta. They make a delicious light meal served with some salad.

1 Squeeze as much water out of the jackfruit as possible and pat dry with kitchen paper (paper towels).

2 Heat 1 tablespoon of the oil in a frying pan (skillet) set over a medium heat and cook the onion and 2 of the garlic cloves, stirring occasionally, for 6–8 minutes until tender. Stir in the jackfruit, maple syrup and stock and simmer for 10 minutes, or until the liquid has been absorbed. Stir in the smoked paprika and set aside.

3 Meanwhile, if you have a spiralizer, you can spiralize the courgettes. Alternatively, use a julienne peeler. If you use a mandolin slicer, you will have thicker 'noodles'.

4 Heat the remaining oil in a pan set over a medium heat and cook the remaining garlic for 2 minutes without browning. Add the white wine, lemon zest and juice and some of the parsley and bring to the boil. Reduce the heat and let it bubble away for 5 minutes, or until reduced. Stir in the pesto and the spiralized courgettes and heat through gently for 2 minutes until the courgettes are just tender. Add the plum tomatoes and season to taste.

5 Divide between 4 serving bowls and top with the jackfruit. Sprinkle with the rest of the parsley and some Parmesan and serve.

OR YOU CAN TRY THIS...
– Serve the pesto and jackfruit with cooked spaghetti or linguine.
– Use vegan pesto, vegan wine and grated cheese.

JACKFRUIT 'CHICKEN' NOODLE SOUP

SERVES: 4 | **PREP:** 15 MINUTES | **COOK:** 20 MINUTES

1 green chilli

2 lemongrass stalks, peeled and chopped

2 garlic cloves, peeled

1 tsp grated fresh root ginger

grated zest and juice of 1 lime

a bunch of fresh coriander (cilantro)

150g/5oz thin rice noodles

2 tbsp vegetable oil

a bunch of spring onions (scallions), thickly sliced

400g/14oz can green jackfruit in brine, drained, rinsed and shredded

1 tsp crushed coriander seeds

750ml/25fl oz (3 cups) hot vegetable stock (broth)

400ml/14fl oz can coconut milk

1 tbsp nam pla (Thai fish sauce)

2 kaffir lime leaves, finely shredded

200g/7oz baby spinach leaves

1 red bird's-eye chilli, deseeded and shredded

Canned jackfruit replaces chicken in this spicy coconut-flavoured soup. This makes enough soup for four, but you can cool and freeze portions if you wish, or store in an airtight container in the fridge to reheat the following day. Vegans can substitute vegan fish sauce or tamari or soy sauce for the nam pla.

1 Blitz the green chilli, lemongrass, garlic, ginger, lime zest and coriander (keep a few sprigs to garnish) to a thick green paste in a mini food processor or blender.

2 Put the rice noodles in a large, shallow heatproof bowl and cover with boiling water. Set aside to soak for 10 minutes, stirring occasionally to prevent them sticking together. (Or follow the instructions on the packet.)

3 Meanwhile, heat the oil in a large saucepan set over a medium heat. Add the spring onions and cook for 2 minutes. Stir in the jackfruit and cook for 5 minutes. Stir in the green paste and crushed coriander seeds and cook for 1 minute, then add the hot vegetable stock, coconut milk, nam pla and kaffir lime leaves. Simmer gently for 10 minutes.

4 Stir in the lime juice and spinach and cook for 1 minute, or just long enough for the spinach to wilt into the soup and turn bright green.

5 Drain the rice noodles and divide between 4 shallow serving bowls. Pour the hot soup over the top and sprinkle with the reserved coriander and shredded chilli. Serve immediately.

OR YOU CAN TRY THIS...

– Use fresh basil instead of coriander.
– Add some shredded carrots, sliced sugar snap peas or shiitake mushrooms.

MEXICAN JACKFRUIT, BEAN & TORTILLA SOUP

SERVES: 6 | **PREP:** 15 MINUTES | **COOK:** 50 MINUTES

3 tbsp olive oil
2 onions, diced
1 large carrot, diced
1 celery stick, diced
3 garlic cloves, crushed
1 red chilli, diced
1 tsp ground cumin
1 tsp smoked paprika
2 x 400g/14oz cans green
   jackfruit in brine, drained,
   rinsed and shredded
1.2 litres/2 pints (5 cups)
   hot vegetable stock (broth)
400g/14oz can chopped
   tomatoes
2 tbsp tomato purée (paste)
1 tbsp sugar
400g/14oz can black beans,
   rinsed and drained
juice of ½ lime
salt and freshly ground
   black pepper

To serve:
a few sprigs of coriander
   (cilantro), chopped
100g/3½oz lightly salted
   tortilla chips, lightly
   crushed
100g/3½oz (1 cup) grated
   Cheddar cheese

The jackfruit adds some interesting 'meaty' texture to this spicy soup. Instead of using tortilla chips, you can cut some soft tortillas into strips, brush with olive oil and bake in a hot oven for 5 minutes until crisp and golden. Lay them on top of the soup.

1 Heat the oil in a large saucepan set over a low to medium heat. Cook the onions, carrot, celery and garlic, stirring occasionally, for 6–8 minutes, or until tender. Stir in the chilli, cumin and smoked paprika and cook for 1 minute. Add the jackfruit and cook for 5 minutes.

2 Pour in the stock and add the tomatoes, tomato purée and sugar. Bring to the boil, then reduce the heat and add the black beans. Simmer gently for 30 minutes. Squeeze in the lime juice and season to taste with salt and pepper.

3 Ladle the hot soup into bowls and sprinkle with the coriander and tortilla chips. Scatter the grated cheese over the top and serve immediately.

OR YOU CAN TRY THIS...
– Use red kidney beans instead of black beans.
– Add some chopped chipotle peppers in adobo sauce.
– Add some fiery heat by adding chilli powder or sprinkling with Tabasco.

TERIYAKI JACKFRUIT & GREENS SUSHI BOWL

SERVES: 4 | **PREP:** 15 MINUTES | **COOK:** 20 MINUTES

2 x 400g/14oz cans green
   jackfruit in brine, drained
   and rinsed
2 tsp olive oil
4 tbsp vegan teriyaki sauce
225g/8oz (1 cup) sushi rice
4 tbsp rice vinegar
2 tbsp sugar
½ tsp salt
500g/1lb 2oz spinach or
   spring greens, washed
   and trimmed
125g/4½oz (generous 1½
   cups) frozen edamame
   (soy) beans
1 large ripe avocado, peeled,
   stoned (pitted) and cubed
4 tsp pickled sushi ginger
1 sheet ready-toasted sushi
   nori, cut into thin shreds
2 tbsp sesame seeds

If you're a fan of sushi, these healthy bowls of jackfruit in teriyaki sauce with beans, avocado, greens and rice could become a firm favourite.

1 Squeeze as much water out of the jackfruit as possible and pat dry with kitchen paper (paper towels).

2 Heat the oil in a large frying pan (skillet) set over a medium heat and cook the jackfruit, stirring occasionally, for 5 minutes. Stir in 4 tablespoons water and 1 tablespoon of the teriyaki sauce and cook for 10–15 minutes until lightly coloured and all the liquid has been absorbed. Shred the jackfruit with 2 forks and stir in the remaining teriyaki sauce.

3 Meanwhile, cook the sushi rice according to the packet instructions. Heat the rice vinegar, sugar and salt in a small saucepan set over a low to medium heat and stir gently until the sugar has dissolved. Sprinkle this over the cooked rice and fork through gently.

4 Put the spinach or greens and 1 tablespoon water into a large saucepan. Cover and cook over a medium heat, shaking the pan occasionally, for 2–3 minutes until the spinach wilts and turns bright green. Drain in a colander, pressing down on the spinach to squeeze out all the moisture.

5 Cook the edamame beans in a saucepan of boiling water for 3 minutes. Refresh under running cold water and then drain.

6 Divide the rice between 4 bowls and top with the teriyaki jackfruit. Add the spinach, edamame beans and avocado to the bowls, then sprinkle with the ginger, shredded nori and sesame seeds. Serve immediately.

OR YOU CAN TRY THIS...
– Drizzle some soy sauce or hot sauce over the top.
– Substitute steamed broccoli for the spinach.

MAIN MEALS

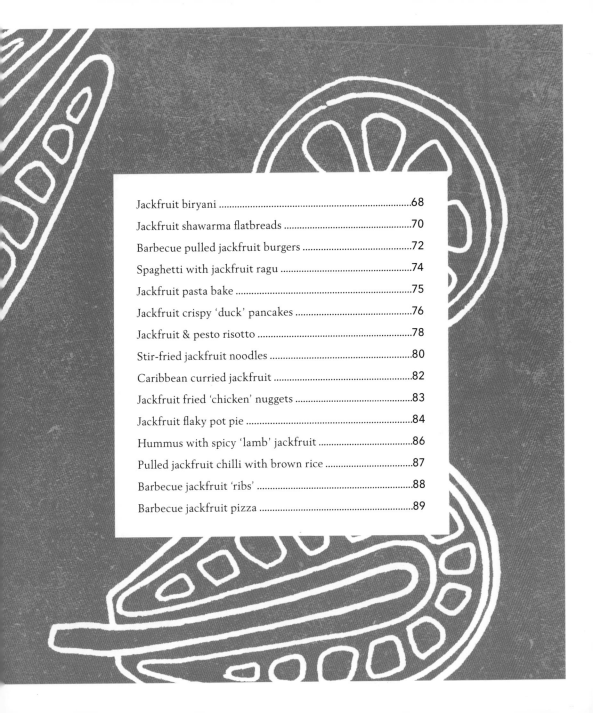

JACKFRUIT BIRIYANI

SERVES: 4 | **PREP:** 25 MINUTES | **MARINATE:** 30 MINUTES | **COOK:** 50 MINUTES

2 x 400g/14oz cans green
   jackfruit in brine, drained
   and rinsed
4 garlic cloves, crushed
1 tbsp ginger purée
½ tsp chilli powder
½ tsp ground turmeric
1 tsp curry paste
300g/10oz (1¼ cups)
   uncooked basmati rice
½ tsp salt
2 cardamom pods
vegetable oil, for deep-frying
180g/6oz (¾ cup) coconut
   yoghurt
1 tsp ground cumin
1 tsp garam masala
2.5cm/1in piece fresh root
   ginger, peeled and diced
2 green chillies, thinly sliced
a handful of coriander
   (cilantro), chopped, plus
   extra to garnish
juice of ½ lime
250g/9oz sweet potatoes,
   peeled and diced
1 red (bell) pepper,
   deseeded and chopped
pinch of saffron strands

continued opposite →

We've given this classic Indian dish a vegan twist by using dairy-free yoghurt, nut milk and coconut oil. Serve it with a crisp salad and some spicy chutney or a cooling vegan raita on the side.

1 Squeeze any liquid out of the jackfruit pieces and pat dry with kitchen paper (paper towels). Cut each piece into 2 or 3 slices and place in a bowl with 2 garlic cloves, the ginger, chilli powder, turmeric, curry paste and 1 tablespoon water. Leave to marinate for 30 minutes.

2 Meanwhile, soak the rice in a bowl of water for 30 minutes, then drain in a sieve and rinse until the water runs clear. Transfer to a saucepan and add the salt and cardamom pods. Cover with plenty of water and bring to the boil. Boil for 8–10 minutes until just tender but not soft (al dente). Drain well.

3 Heat the oil for deep-frying in a deep fryer or heavy saucepan; when it reaches 170°C/340°F, add the jackfruit and cook for 4–5 minutes, in batches (don't overcrowd the pan), until crispy and golden brown. Remove and drain on kitchen paper (paper towels).

4 Preheat the oven to 200°C, 400°F, gas mark 6.

5 Blitz the yoghurt with the cumin, garam masala, ginger, chillies, remaining garlic cloves, coriander and lime juice in a blender. Transfer to a flameproof casserole and stir in the diced sweet potato and red pepper. Set over a low to medium heat and cook gently for 5 minutes. Spoon the jackfruit over the top and cover with the drained rice. Stir the saffron into the warmed milk and drizzle over the top with the coconut oil. Tightly cover the casserole with 2 layers of foil and the lid, then cook in the oven for 25–30 minutes.

6 Meanwhile, deep-fry the onions in a pan of hot oil until crisp and golden brown. Drain on kitchen paper.

2 tbsp almond milk, warmed
30g/1oz (2 tbsp) coconut
oil, melted
2 large onions, sliced in rings
sultanas (golden raisins) and
flaked almonds, to serve

7 Serve the biriyani topped with the deep-fried onions, chopped
coriander, sultanas and almonds.

....

OR YOU CAN TRY THIS...

– Vary the vegetables: try cauliflower, beetroot (beets), green beans,
carrots and peas.
– Use fresh mint instead of coriander.

JACKFRUIT SHAWARMA FLATBREADS

SERVES: 4 | **PREP:** 20 MINUTES | **CHILL:** 1 HOUR | **COOK:** 25-30 MINUTES

2 x 400g/14oz cans green jackfruit in brine, drained and rinsed
1 tsp fennel seeds
240g/8oz (1 cup) coconut or soya yoghurt
a few fennel fronds, finely chopped
a squeeze of lemon juice
1–2 tsp harissa paste
4 large flatbreads or pitta breads (see Tip)
4 heaped tbsp hummus
4 tomatoes, roughly chopped
½ red onion, diced
pickled cucumbers or hot chillies, to serve

Spicy, aromatic shawarma dishes are popular throughout the Middle East. They're usually made with chicken or lamb, but you can make your 'meaty' vegan version with jackfruit. The traditional accompaniment is a pungent garlic sauce, but we've used fennel-flavoured yoghurt with a dash of fiery red harissa.

1 Cut the jackfruit into thin slices and pat dry with kitchen paper (paper towels). Place in a bowl with all the shawarma marinade ingredients. Give them a good stir, then cover and chill in the fridge for at least 1 hour.

2 Preheat the oven to 190°C, 375°F, gas mark 5. Line a baking tray (cookie sheet) with baking parchment.

3 Arrange the marinated jackfruit on the lined baking tray and bake for 25–30 minutes, or until crisp and golden brown and beginning to char, turning the jackfruit halfway through. Shred with 2 forks.

4 Meanwhile, heat a small frying pan (skillet) set over a high heat. Add the fennel seeds and cook for about 1 minute, tossing occasionally, until golden brown and they release their aroma. Remove from the pan immediately before they burn and stir into the yoghurt with the chopped fennel and lemon juice. Swirl in the harissa.

5 Warm the flatbreads on both sides in a griddle (grill) pan set over a medium heat. Spread the flatbreads with hummus and add the tomatoes and red onion. Cover with the jackfruit and add some pickled cucumbers or chillies. Top with the fennel and harissa yoghurt and fold the flatbread over the top. Serve immediately.

For the shawarma marinade:
3 tbsp olive oil
juice of ½ lemon
2 garlic cloves, crushed
1 tsp cumin seeds, crushed
1 tsp sumac
½ tsp ras el hanout
½ tsp ground turmeric
½ tsp smoked paprika
pinch of ground cinnamon
a few sprigs of parsley,
    chopped
salt and freshly ground
    black pepper

OR YOU CAN TRY THIS...
– Add some shredded lettuce, diced cucumber and chickpeas.
– If you're not vegan, add some diced feta.
– Serve drizzled with tahini or hot sauce.
– Stir some diced fennel bulb or cucumber into the yoghurt.

TIP: If using pittas, cut them open down one side with a sharp knife and fill with all the topping ingredients.

BARBECUE PULLED JACKFRUIT BURGERS

SERVES: 4 | **PREP:** 20 MINUTES | **COOK:** 20 MINUTES

olive oil, for brushing
2 x 400g/14oz cans green
    jackfruit in brine, drained
    and rinsed
120ml/4fl oz (½ cup)
    barbecue sauce
4 ciabatta rolls or burger buns
1 large ripe avocado, peeled,
    stoned (pitted) and
    mashed
1 beef tomato, thinly sliced
crisps (potato chips) or fries,
    to serve

For the coleslaw:
¼ white or red cabbage,
    cored and thinly
    shredded
½ onion, grated
2 carrots, grated
4–5 tbsp mayonnaise
1 tsp mustard
a handful of parsley,
    finely chopped
60g/2¼oz (½ cup)
    chopped walnuts
lemon juice, to taste

These tangy burgers make a quick and easy supper. And if you have meat-eating guests, they will be amazed at how similar the jackfruit looks and tastes to pulled pork. You can make the crunchy coleslaw in advance and keep in the fridge for up to 3 days. If you're vegan, use vegan mayo and vegan-friendly barbecue sauce.

1 Preheat the oven to 200°C, 400°F, gas mark 6. Line a baking tray (cookie sheet) with foil and brush lightly with olive oil.

2 Squeeze any liquid out of the jackfruit pieces and pat dry with kitchen paper (paper towels). Shred them with 2 forks and place in a bowl with the barbecue sauce. Mix well to coat all the jackfruit strands.

3 Spread the jackfruit out in a single layer on the lined baking tray and bake in the oven for about 20 minutes, or until the jackfruit is crisp and browned.

4 Meanwhile, make the coleslaw: put the cabbage, onion and carrots into a bowl and mix with the mayonnaise and mustard until everything is lightly coated. Stir in the parsley and walnuts and some lemon juice.

5 Split the ciabatta rolls and lightly toast them. Spread the bases with the mashed avocado and cover with the tomato slices. Pile the jackfruit on top, then add the coleslaw. Cover with the ciabatta tops and serve immediately with some crisps or fries.

OR YOU CAN TRY THIS...
– Serve with tomato ketchup or hot salsa.
– Use chopped cashews or pecans instead of walnuts.
– Instead of a roll, put everything in a tortilla or wrap.

SPAGHETTI WITH JACKFRUIT RAGU

SERVES: 4 | **PREP:** 15 MINUTES | **COOK:** 45 MINUTES

2 x 400g/14oz cans green
    jackfruit in brine, drained
    and rinsed
2 tbsp olive oil, plus extra
    for the pasta
1 large onion, diced
4 garlic cloves, crushed
2 carrots, diced
2 celery sticks, finely
    chopped
1 tsp dried oregano
1 tsp chopped thyme
60ml/2fl oz (¼ cup)
    almond milk
210ml/7fl oz (scant 1 cup)
    vegan-friendly red wine
400g/14oz can chopped
    tomatoes
2 tbsp tomato purée (paste)
2 tsp sugar
1 tbsp balsamic vinegar
1 bay leaf
a few sprigs of fresh basil
    leaves, torn
500g/1lb 2oz dried
    spaghetti
salt and freshly ground
    black pepper
grated vegan Parmesan,
    for sprinkling

Shredded jackfruit works well in this classic ragu sauce with a vegan twist. It keeps well in the fridge for 24 hours, so you can make it in advance and reheat it the following day. Alternatively, double the quantities and allow to cool before freezing.

1 Squeeze any liquid out from the jackfruit pieces and pat dry with kitchen paper (paper towels). Cut each piece into 2–3 slices.

2 Heat the olive oil in a large saucepan set over a medium heat. Add the jackfruit and cook, stirring occasionally, for 8–10 minutes until coloured and starting to caramelize. Squash with a spoon or shred coarsely with 2 forks. Stir in the onion, garlic, carrots and celery and cook for 6–8 minutes, or until tender.

3 Add the oregano, thyme and almond milk and cook for 5 minutes, or until the milk is absorbed. Stir in the red wine, tomatoes, tomato purée, sugar and balsamic vinegar and bring to the boil. Reduce the heat, add the bay leaf and cook gently for 20 minutes, or until the vegetables are cooked and the sauce has reduced a little. If the sauce is too thick, thin it down with some of the cooking water from the pasta (see below). Discard the bay leaf, season to taste with salt and pepper and stir in the basil.

4 Meanwhile, cook the spaghetti according to the packet instructions. Drain well and toss in a little olive oil.

5 Toss the spaghetti in the sauce and serve in shallow bowls sprinkled with grated vegan Parmesan.

OR YOU CAN TRY THIS...
– Use linguine, tagliatelle or pappardelle instead of spaghetti.
– For a stronger flavour, add some soy sauce or Marmite.
– Add some mushrooms or fresh tomatoes.

JACKFRUIT PASTA BAKE

VEGAN

SERVES: 4 | **PREP:** 10 MINUTES | **COOK:** 55-60 MINUTES

250g/9oz dried pasta shapes,
 e.g. penne or fusilli
2 tbsp olive oil
1 onion, diced
2 garlic cloves, crushed
2 red or yellow (bell)
 peppers, deseeded and
 chopped
300g/10oz mushrooms,
 halved or sliced
400g/14oz can green
 jackfruit in brine,
 drained and rinsed
1 tsp Italian seasoning
2 x 400g/14oz cans chopped
 tomatoes
1 tbsp tomato purée (paste)
2 tsp sugar
200g/7oz baby spinach leaves
100g/3½oz (1 cup)
 shredded vegan cheese
salt and freshly ground
 black pepper
freshly chopped parsley
 or basil leaves, to serve

This tasty pasta bake is packed with healthy vegetables and dietary fibre, making it very gut-friendly. You could batch-cook it at the weekend and pop some in the freezer for an easy supper at a later date.

1 Preheat the oven to 190°C, 375°F, gas mark 5.

2 Cook the pasta according to the packet instructions. Drain well.

3 Heat the olive oil in a large frying pan (skillet) set over a medium heat and cook the onion, garlic and peppers, stirring occasionally, for 5 minutes. Stir in the mushrooms and cook for a further 5 minutes, or until golden brown.

4 Meanwhile, squeeze any liquid out of the jackfruit pieces and pat dry with kitchen paper (paper towels).

5 Add the jackfruit and Italian seasoning to the pan and cook, stirring occasionally, for 8–10 minutes until they start to caramelize. Squash with a spoon or shred coarsely with 2 forks. Stir in the tomatoes, tomato purée and sugar, then reduce the heat and simmer gently for about 15 minutes. Stir in the spinach and cook for 1 minute. Season to taste and stir in the cooked pasta.

6 Transfer to a baking dish, sprinkle the vegan cheese over the top and bake for 20–25 minutes, or until bubbling and golden brown. Serve, sprinkled with parsley or basil, with a crisp salad.

OR YOU CAN TRY THIS...
– Add diced courgette (zucchini), shredded kale or broccoli florets.
– Add some fresh herbs, e.g. thyme, marjoram or oregano.
– Stir in some stoned (pitted) black olives.

JACKFRUIT CRISPY 'DUCK' PANCAKES

SERVES: 4 | **PREP:** 20 MINUTES | **COOK:** 35 MINUTES

2 x 400g/14oz cans green
    jackfruit in brine, drained
    and rinsed
2 tbsp vegetable, olive or
    groundnut (peanut) oil
3 garlic cloves, crushed
2.5cm/1in piece fresh root
    ginger, peeled and diced
1 tsp five-spice powder
1 tsp whole Szechuan
    peppercorns, crushed
¼ tsp ground cinnamon
3 tbsp hoisin sauce
1 tbsp soy sauce or tamari
1 tsp toasted sesame oil
1 tsp rice vinegar
16 Chinese pancakes

To serve:
½ cucumber, cut into thin
    matchsticks
a bunch of spring onions
    (scallions), white parts
    only, shredded
Szechuan or Chinese plum
    sauce or hoisin sauce

These Chinese crispy 'duck' pancakes are easy to prepare and cook – perfect for entertaining as guests can assemble them themselves. Ready-made pancakes are available in most large supermarkets, Chinese food stores and online.

1 Preheat the oven to 200°C, 400°F, gas mark 6. Line a baking tray (cookie sheet) with baking parchment.

2 Squeeze any liquid out of the jackfruit pieces and pat dry with kitchen paper (paper towels).

3 Heat the oil in a large frying pan (skillet) set over a medium heat. Cook the garlic and ginger for 2–3 minutes without browning. Add the five-spice powder, Szechuan peppercorns and cinnamon and cook for 1 minute. Stir in the jackfruit pieces, hoisin sauce, soy sauce or tamari, sesame oil and vinegar. Reduce the heat and cook gently for 10 minutes. Break the jackfruit up into smaller pieces or shred roughly with 2 forks.

4 Spread the jackfruit out in a single layer on the lined baking tray, spooning any leftover sauce from the pan over the top. Cook in the oven for 20 minutes, or until browned and starting to crisp.

5 Meanwhile, wrap the pancakes in some baking parchment or foil and warm through in a bamboo steamer basket set over a saucepan of simmering water. Alternatively, heat them in a microwave.

6 To serve, arrange the jackfruit on a serving platter with the cucumber and spring onions on the side. Keep the pancakes warm in the steamer or cover with a cloth. Spread the plum or hoisin sauce over the pancakes, sprinkle with cucumber and spring onions, then top with jackfruit and roll up. Delicious!

OR YOU CAN TRY THIS...
– Add some ground star anise to the marinade mixture.

JACKFRUIT & PESTO RISOTTO

SERVES: 4 | **PREP:** 15 MINUTES | **COOK:** 35 MINUTES

900ml/1½ pints (scant
   4 cups) vegetable stock
   (broth)
1 tbsp extra-virgin olive oil
30g/1oz (2 tbsp) butter
a bunch of spring onions
   (scallions), chopped
2 garlic cloves, crushed
2 celery sticks, diced
200g/7oz thin asparagus,
   trimmed and cut into
   5cm/2in pieces
400g/14oz can green
   jackfruit in brine, drained
   and rinsed
good pinch of chilli powder
250g/9oz (scant 1½ cups)
   risotto rice
120ml/4fl oz (½ cup)
   dry white wine or dry
   vermouth
grated zest and juice of
   1 lemon
2 handfuls of mixed herbs,
   e.g. parsley, basil or
   chives, chopped
120ml/4fl oz (½ cup) fresh
   green pesto
30g/1oz (¼ cup) grated
   Parmesan cheese
salt and freshly ground
   black pepper

We've added some jackfruit to this lovely green risotto made with spring vegetables and herbs. To make it vegan, use vegan-friendly wine, pesto and shredded cheese and substitute extra oil for the butter.

1 Heat the vegetable stock in a saucepan until it starts to simmer. Leave on a low heat while you make the risotto.

2 Heat the oil and butter in a heavy-based wide saucepan set over a low to medium heat and cook the spring onions, garlic and celery, stirring occasionally, for 5 minutes, or until softened but not coloured. Add the asparagus and cook for 2 minutes.

3 Meanwhile, squeeze any liquid out of the jackfruit pieces and pat dry with kitchen paper (paper towels). Shred them roughly with 2 forks and add to the pan with the chilli powder. Stir well and cook gently for 5 minutes.

4 Add the rice and keep stirring gently until all the grains are glistening and coated with oil. Pour in the wine or vermouth and cook for 4–5 minutes, or until most of the liquid has evaporated.

5 Add a ladle of simmering stock and stir until it has all been absorbed by the rice, then add another ladleful. Keep adding and stirring until all or most of the stock has been used up and the rice is plump and tender with a little bite.

6 Stir in the lemon zest and juice, chopped herbs and pesto. Taste the risotto and add some salt and pepper if required (some pesto is quite salty, so do taste before adding).

7 Divide the risotto between 4 shallow serving bowls or plates and serve sprinkled with grated Parmesan.

OR YOU CAN TRY THIS...

– Add some diced courgette (zucchini), baby spinach leaves, baby leeks or peas.
– Add a pinch of saffron strands to the hot stock and top with pesto instead of stirring it in to the saffron rice.

STIR-FRIED JACKFRUIT NOODLES

SERVES: 4 | **PREP:** 15 MINUTES | **COOK:** 12-15 MINUTES

250g/9oz rice noodles
(dry weight)

2 x 400g/14oz cans green
jackfruit in brine, drained
and rinsed

1 tbsp groundnut (peanut) oil

a bunch of spring onions
(scallions), sliced

1 red (bell) pepper, deseeded
and thinly sliced

2 carrots, cut into
matchsticks

3 garlic cloves, crushed

1 red bird's-eye chilli, diced

1 tsp grated fresh root ginger

2 heads pak choi (bok choy),
sliced

a handful of coriander
(cilantro), chopped

40g/1½oz (½ cup) roasted
peanuts

lime wedges, for squeezing

For the spicy peanut sauce:
5 tbsp crunchy peanut butter

2 tbsp soy sauce or vegan
nam pla (Thai fish sauce)

1 tbsp sesame oil

1 tbsp rice vinegar

2 tsp maple syrup

1 tsp Sriracha

juice of 1 lime

The spicy peanut sauce is easy-peasy to make and gives a creamy finishing touch to this delicious stir fry. It's perfect for a weekday supper.

1 Make the spicy peanut sauce: beat all the ingredients together in a bowl or jug until well blended and creamy.

2 Cook the rice noodles according to the packet instructions and drain.

3 Squeeze any liquid out of the jackfruit pieces and pat dry with kitchen paper (paper towels). Shred roughly with 2 forks.

4 Heat the oil in a wok or deep frying pan (skillet) set over a medium heat. Add the spring onions (scallions), red pepper and carrots and stir-fry for 2 minutes. Stir in the garlic, chilli and ginger and cook for a further 1 minute.

5 Add the jackfruit and stir-fry for 4–5 minutes. Add the pak choi and stir-fry for 2 minutes more. Gently stir in the cooked rice noodles and spicy peanut sauce and toss lightly together. Cook for 1 minute and stir in the coriander.

6 Divide the mixture between 4 serving bowls. Sprinkle with peanuts and serve immediately with some lime wedges for squeezing.

OR YOU CAN TRY THIS...

– Add some tenderstem broccoli, courgette (zucchini) matchsticks or beansprouts.

– Use cashew nut butter instead of peanut butter and sprinkle with chopped salted cashews.

– Add some vegan Thai curry paste and coconut milk to the sauce.

– Substitute Thai basil and mint for the coriander.

CARIBBEAN CURRIED JACKFRUIT

SERVES: 4 | **PREP:** 15 MINUTES | **COOK:** 30-35 MINUTES

2 tbsp coconut oil
1 large onion, thinly sliced
3 garlic cloves, crushed
2.5cm/1in piece fresh root
    ginger, peeled and diced
1 Scotch bonnet chilli, diced
¼ tsp ground allspice
1 tsp ground turmeric
4 sprigs fresh thyme
2 x 400g/14oz cans green
    jackfruit in brine, drained
    and rinsed
4 ripe tomatoes, chopped
400ml/14fl oz can coconut
    milk
2 large sweet potatoes,
    peeled and cubed
1 tsp coconut sugar
100g/3½oz baby spinach
    leaves
1 tbsp black mustard seeds
a handful of coriander
    (cilantro), chopped
salt and freshly ground
    black pepper
boiled rice or rice 'n' peas
    (see page 55), to serve

Jackfruit is widely eaten in the islands of the Caribbean and is often added to curries with yams, sweet potatoes and coconut milk. This spicy dish will bring a touch of sunshine and heat – Scotch bonnet chillies are seriously hot!

1 Heat the oil in a large, deep frying pan (skillet) set over a medium heat. Add the onion, garlic, ginger and chilli to the pan and cook for 4–5 minutes until softened and slightly coloured. Stir in the ground spices and thyme and cook for 1 minute.

2 Squeeze any liquid out of the jackfruit pieces and pat dry with kitchen paper (paper towels). Cut each piece in half and add to the pan. Cook for 4–5 minutes.

3 Add the tomatoes, coconut milk, sweet potatoes and coconut sugar and bring to the boil. Reduce the heat, cover with a lid and cook gently for 15–20 minutes, or until the sweet potatoes are tender, checking from time to time that the curry is not too dry. Add some vegetable stock (broth) or water to moisten it if necessary. Stir in the spinach leaves and cook for 1–2 minutes until they wilt, then season with salt and pepper to taste.

4 Meanwhile, toast the mustard seeds in a small dry frying pan set over a medium to high heat. Within 1–2 minutes they will start popping and release their aroma. Remove from the pan immediately before they burn.

5 Serve the curry sprinkled with the toasted seeds and chopped coriander with some boiled rice or rice 'n' peas on the side.

OR YOU CAN TRY THIS...
– Add some chunks of chayote (christophene) or okra.
– Add some canned chickpeas or black beans.

JACKFRUIT FRIED 'CHICKEN' NUGGETS

SERVES: 3-4 | **PREP:** 15 MINUTES | **MARINATE:** 10-15 MINUTES | **COOK:** 15 MINUTES

2 x 400g/14oz cans green
jackfruit in brine, drained
and rinsed
4 tbsp vegan Dijon mustard
1 tsp dried oregano
240ml/8fl oz (1 cup)
unsweetened almond milk
2 tsp apple cider vinegar
salt and freshly ground
black pepper
vegetable or groundnut
(peanut) oil, for frying

For the coating:
60g/2oz (½ cup) plain
(all-purpose) flour
60g/2oz (½ cup) cornflour
(cornstarch)
1 tsp baking powder
1 tsp smoked paprika
½ tsp garlic powder
¼ tsp cayenne
150g/5oz (1½ cups) dried
breadcrumbs

To serve:
vegan mayo or hot sauce
lemon wedges

This is just another example of how versatile jackfruit is. The nuggets don't take much time to prepare and they are cooked in minutes. You can serve them as a main course for all the family with potatoes, rice or grains, plus a salad or vegetables and all your favourite sauces, dips or condiments.

1 Gently squeeze any liquid out of the jackfruit pieces and pat dry with kitchen paper (paper towels). Brush them with the mustard and sprinkle with oregano.

2 Whisk the almond milk, cider vinegar and some seasoning in a bowl and gently stir in the jackfruit pieces. Leave to marinate for 10–15 minutes.

3 For the coating, mix together the flour, cornflour, baking powder and spices in a shallow bowl. Put in the breadcrumbs in another shallow bowl or on a deep plate.

4 Remove the jackfruit pieces from the marinade (reserving it) and dip them into the flour mixture to coat them lightly all over. Shake off the excess and quickly dip them into the reserved marinade, then coat with the breadcrumbs.

5 Pour enough oil into a large pan to give a depth of 1cm/½in. Set over a medium to high heat; when it's really hot, add the nuggets, a few at a time. Fry, turning them occasionally, for 3–4 minutes each side, until crisp and golden brown. Remove and drain on kitchen paper.

6 Serve them piping hot with vegan mayo or hot sauce and lemon wedges for squeezing. A crisp salad or steamed green vegetables and some rice make a good accompaniment.

JACKFRUIT FLAKY POT PIE

SERVES: 4 | **PREP:** 15 MINUTES | **COOK:** 45-50 MINUTES

2 tbsp olive oil
1 onion, diced
2 garlic cloves, crushed
2 leeks, washed, trimmed
    and sliced
2 sweet potatoes, peeled
    and cubed
400g/14oz can green
    jackfruit in brine, drained
    and rinsed
1 tsp thyme leaves
150g/5oz (1 cup) frozen peas
1 ready-rolled puff
    pastry sheet
1 tsp butter, melted

For the white sauce:
2 tbsp olive oil
45g/1½oz (scant ½ cup)
    plain (all-purpose) flour
480ml/16fl oz (2 cups)
    unsweetened almond
    milk, warmed
good pinch of nutmeg
salt and freshly ground
    black pepper

This creamy vegetable pie is great for supper on a cold day. If you're vegan, use vegan puff pastry and vegan butter. You could also divide the filling between 4 small individual pie dishes or ramekins instead of making one large pie.

1 Preheat the oven to 200°C, 400°F, gas mark 6.

2 Heat the oil in a large saucepan set over a medium heat. Add the onion, garlic, leeks, sweet potatoes, jackfruit and thyme and stir well. Cover the pan with a lid and cook for 10 minutes, or until softened.

3 Make the white sauce: heat the olive oil in a saucepan set over a medium heat and stir in the flour until it combines to make a smooth ball. Add a splash of the warm almond milk and whisk until combined. Beat in the remaining milk, a little at a time, until smooth and free from lumps. Stir continuously until it comes to the boil and the sauce thickens. Season to taste with nutmeg, salt and pepper.

4 Mix the cooked vegetables and the peas into the white sauce and pour into an ovenproof pie dish. Brush the rim of the dish with a little water and cover with the pastry, pressing it down around the rim. Trim off any excess pastry and crimp the edges with a fork or your fingers. Cut a small cross in the top to allow the steam to escape and brush lightly with the melted butter.

5 Bake in the oven for 25–30 minutes until the pastry is crisp and golden brown. Serve hot.

OR YOU CAN TRY THIS...

– Use potato or butternut squash instead of sweet potato.
– Add some sliced mushrooms or carrots.

HUMMUS WITH SPICY 'LAMB' JACKFRUIT

SERVES: 4 | **PREP:** 10 MINUTES | **COOK:** 20 MINUTES

4 tbsp olive oil
2 onions, thinly sliced
3 garlic cloves, crushed
1 tbsp ras el hanout
2 tsp ground cumin
1 tsp paprika
½ tsp ground turmeric
½ tsp ground allspice
½ tsp ground cinnamon
1 tsp dried chilli flakes
2 x 400g/14oz cans green
    jackfruit in brine, drained
    and rinsed
1 tbsp tomato purée (paste)
2 x 400g/14oz cans chopped
    tomatoes
400g/14oz can chickpeas,
    drained
1 tbsp pomegranate molasses
1 tsp maple syrup
200g/7oz (scant 1 cup)
    hummus
salt and freshly ground
    black pepper
a handful of flat-leaf parsley,
    chopped
pomegranate seeds and
    toasted pine nuts,
    for sprinkling
4 warm pitta breads,
    cut into triangles
lemon wedges, to serve

In the Levant, hummus is often served topped with spiced lamb or vegetables. In this delicious recipe, we've used jackfruit instead.

1 Heat the olive oil in a large heavy-based frying pan (skillet) set over a low heat and cook the onions and garlic very slowly for about 15 minutes until tender, golden brown and starting to caramelize. Stir in the spices and chilli flakes and cook for 1 minute.

2 Meanwhile, squeeze any liquid out of the jackfruit and pat dry with kitchen paper (paper towels). Add to the pan and cook over a medium heat for 5 minutes. Stir in the tomato purée, chopped tomatoes and chickpeas and cook for 10–15 minutes until thickened and reduced. Add the pomegranate molasses and maple syrup and season to taste.

3 Smear the hummus round 4 serving plates in a circle. Pile the jackfruit mixture into the centre of each circle and scatter with the parsley, pomegranate seeds and toasted pine nuts. Serve immediately with warm pitta bread and lemon wedges.

OR YOU CAN TRY THIS...

– Swap the toasted pine nuts for chopped pistachios.
– Serve with couscous instead of hummus.
– Use mint or coriander (cilantro) instead of parsley.
– Add some dried apricots or prunes to the jackfruit.

PULLED JACKFRUIT CHILLI WITH BROWN RICE

SERVES: 4 | **PREP:** 15 MINUTES | **COOK:** 45-50 MINUTES

1 tbsp coconut oil
1 large red onion, chopped
3 garlic cloves, crushed
2 carrots, diced
2 celery sticks, diced
1 red (bell) pepper, deseeded and chopped
2 tsp chilli powder
2 tsp smoked paprika
400g/14oz can green jackfruit in brine, drained and rinsed
2 x 400g/14oz cans chopped tomatoes
2 tbsp tomato purée (paste)
1 tsp dried thyme
2 x 400g/14oz cans kidney beans, drained
1 tbsp soy sauce
1 tbsp coconut sugar
250g/9oz (generous 1 cup) brown rice
salt and freshly ground black pepper

To serve:
1 avocado, peeled, stoned (pitted) and diced
juice of 1 lime
vegan sour cream, to serve

Pulled jackfruit makes a great substitute for minced beef in our fabulous vegan chilli. It's filling and great for warming you up on a cold winter's day. Serve it at parties and for Halloween.

1 Heat the oil in a large saucepan set over a low to medium heat. Cook the onion, garlic, carrots, celery and red pepper, stirring occasionally, for 8–10 minutes until tender. Stir in the chilli powder and paprika and cook for 2 minutes.

2 Squeeze any liquid out of the jackfruit pieces and pat dry with kitchen paper (paper towels). Use 2 forks to shred the jackfruit and add to the pan. Cook for 4–5 minutes.

3 Add the tomatoes, tomato purée, thyme, kidney beans, soy sauce and coconut sugar. Stir well and simmer gently over a low heat for 30 minutes, or until the sauce reduces and thickens. Season to taste with salt and pepper.

4 Meanwhile, cook the rice according to the packet instructions.

5 Serve the chilli with the brown rice, some avocado tossed in lime juice and a dollop of vegan sour cream.

OR YOU CAN TRY THIS...
– Add some cayenne pepper, a dash of balsamic vinegar or aminos (liquid smoke).
– Sprinkle with chopped coriander (cilantro).
– Serve with guacamole and lime wedges for squeezing.
– Add some more heat with a diced fresh chilli or a dash of hot sauce.

TIP: You can buy dairy-free sour cream at most large supermarkets and health food and wholefood stores.

BARBECUE JACKFRUIT 'RIBS'

SERVES: 4 | **PREP:** 20 MINUTES | **COOK:** 50-55 MINUTES

1 tbsp coconut oil, plus extra for oiling

2 x 400g/14oz cans green jackfruit in brine, drained and rinsed

1 red onion, diced

4 garlic cloves, crushed

1 tbsp smoked paprika

½ tsp ground cumin

¼ tsp ground allspice

¼ tsp crushed chilli flakes

1 tbsp tomato purée (paste)

2 tbsp smooth peanut butter

1 tbsp maple syrup

2 tbsp soy sauce

2–3 drops aminos (liquid smoke)

180ml/6fl oz (¾ cup) vegetable stock (broth)

150g/5oz (1¼ cups) vital wheat gluten

25g/1oz (⅓ cup) chickpea (gram) flour

2 tbsp nutritional yeast

240ml/8fl oz (1 cup) vegan-friendly barbecue sauce

4 pieces of corn on the cob, to serve

vegan potato salad, to serve

The nutritional yeast adds a savoury, nutty flavour while the vital wheat gluten helps to give the 'ribs' a meaty texture.

1 Preheat the oven to 190°C, 375°F, gas mark 5. Lightly oil a 20cm/8in square baking pan. Squeeze any liquid out of the jackfruit and pat dry with kitchen paper (paper towels).

2 Heat the oil in a frying pan (skillet) set over a medium heat and cook the red onion and garlic, stirring occasionally, for 6–8 minutes until softened. Add the jackfruit and cook for 10 minutes. Stir in the spices, chilli flakes and tomato purée and cook for 1 minute. Use a potato masher to shred the jackfruit.

3 Transfer to a bowl and stir in the peanut butter, maple syrup, soy sauce, aminos and vegetable stock.

4 In another large bowl, mix together the vital wheat gluten, chickpea flour and nutritional yeast. Add the jackfruit mixture, mixing until you have a soft ball of dough. If it's too wet, add more vital wheat gluten; if it's too dry, add more stock.

5 Knead the dough for 5 minutes until it holds together. Flatten with a rolling pin to make a 2.5cm/1in thick rectangle and place in the baking pan. Bake for 20–25 minutes, then turn out onto a board and brush the top with some of the barbecue sauce.

6 Preheat the barbecue or heat an oiled, ridged griddle (grill) pan set over a medium heat. Place the ribs, sauce side down, on the hot griddle and cook for 5 minutes, or until browned and striped underneath. Pour the remaining barbecue sauce over the top and flip over. Cook the other side until browned. Transfer to a board and cut into 'ribs'. Serve with corn on the cob and potato salad.

OR YOU CAN TRY THIS...
– Serve with garlic mashed potato or guacamole.

BARBECUE JACKFRUIT PIZZA

SERVES: 4 | **PREP:** 20 MINUTES | **COOK:** 30 MINUTES

4 tbsp olive oil

3 red onions, thinly sliced

2 tbsp fennel seeds

4 tbsp pine nuts

45g/1½oz (¼ cup) sultanas (golden raisins)

a few drops of balsamic vinegar

400g/14oz can green jackfruit in brine, drained and rinsed

120ml/4fl oz (½ cup) barbecue sauce

1 tbsp maple syrup

4–5 tbsp tomato purée (paste)

150g/5oz mozzarella, sliced

salt and freshly ground black pepper

For the easy pizza dough:
450g/1lb (4½ cups) strong white bread flour

1 x 7g/¼oz sachet fast-action yeast

1 tsp caster (superfine) sugar

1 tsp sea salt

2 tbsp olive oil

240ml/8fl oz (1 cup) warm water

If you don't want to make dough, you can buy ready-made rolled dough or fresh or frozen pizza bases.

1 Preheat the oven to 230°C, 450°F, gas mark 8.

2 Make the pizza dough: put the flour, yeast, sugar and salt into a bowl and mix together. Make a well in the centre and pour in the olive oil and water. Mix to a soft dough, drawing in flour from the sides with your hand. If the dough is too dry, add a little more warm water. Turn out onto a floured surface and knead for 2–3 minutes into a smooth ball. Cover and set aside.

3 Heat 3 tablespoons of the oil in a large frying pan (skillet) set over a low heat. Cook the onions, stirring occasionally, for 15 minutes, or until golden and starting to caramelize. Stir in the fennel seeds and cook for 1 minute, then add the pine nuts and sultanas. Add the balsamic vinegar and salt and pepper to taste.

4 Meanwhile, squeeze any liquid out of the jackfruit and pat dry with kitchen paper (paper towels). Heat the remaining oil in a saucepan set over a medium heat, add the jackfruit and cook for 5 minutes. Add the barbecue sauce and maple syrup and cook for a further 10 minutes. Shred the jackfruit with 2 forks.

5 Divide the pizza dough into 2 portions and roll out each one thinly into a large circle. Place on 2 baking trays (cookie sheets). Spread the tomato purée thinly over them, leaving a border around the edge, and spoon the onion mixture on top. Scatter with mozzarella and add the barbecue jackfruit.

6 Bake in the oven for 12–15 minutes until the cheese has melted, the crust is golden and the jackfruit is starting to crisp.

OR YOU CAN TRY THIS...

– Add some diced chilli, pineapple chunks or sweetcorn kernels.

DESSERTS, PRESERVES & DRINKS

TROPICAL JACKFRUIT POPSICLES

MAKES: 8 | **PREP:** 15 MINUTES | **FREEZE:** 8 HOURS+

250g/9oz frozen ripe, sweet jackfruit, deseeded
150g/5oz fresh mango, peeled, stoned (pitted) and cubed
1 frozen banana
200ml/7fl oz (scant 1 cup) canned full-fat coconut milk
180ml/6fl oz (¾ cup) pineapple juice

We haven't added sugar or sweetener to these creamy popsicles, but if you have a really sweet tooth, you could stir in some honey (if you're not vegan) or natural stevia to taste. It's best to use silicone popsicle moulds as the frozen pops turn out really easily – buy them online and in specialist kitchen stores.

1 Blitz all the ingredients in a blender until thick, creamy and smooth.

2 Pour the mixture into 8 popsicle moulds and insert some wooden sticks. Freeze for at least 8 hours or, better still, overnight, until the popsicles are frozen solid.

3 To turn out the popsicles, run the moulds under hot water for a few seconds, taking care not to let the water get inside the moulds. You can keep these pops frozen for up to 1 month.

OR YOU CAN TRY THIS...
– Use a mixture of jackfruit and papaya (pawpaw) or pineapple.
– Add a few drops of vanilla extract.
– Add some shredded ripe jackfruit to the purée for texture.
– Stir in some chia seeds or coconut shreds.

FROZEN JACKFRUIT MARGARITA SORBET VEGAN

SERVES: 6 | **PREP:** 15 MINUTES | **FREEZE:** 4-6 HOURS

450g/1lb (3 cups) fresh ripe, sweet jackfruit, deseeded and chopped
120ml/4fl oz (½ cup) tequila
80ml/3fl oz (⅓ cup) triple sec
240ml/8fl oz (1 cup) orange or pineapple juice
1 tbsp agave nectar
lime wedges
coarse sea salt, for the edges of glasses

Jackfruit imparts a sweet, tropical flavour to frozen margarita sorbets and cocktails. These desserts look pretty served in salt-rimmed glasses or dishes.

1 Blitz the jackfruit, tequila, triple sec, fruit juice and agave in a blender until smooth.

2 Pour into a plastic container, cover tightly with cling film (plastic wrap) and freeze for 4–6 hours.

3 When you're ready to serve the sorbet, rub the lime wedges around the rims of 6 glasses or small glass dishes and dip them into a saucer of sea salt, so it sticks to the rims. Scoop out the sorbet into the glasses or bowls and serve immediately.

4 This keeps in the freezer in a sealed plastic container for up to 2 weeks.

OR YOU CAN TRY THIS...
– Add agave nectar to taste – you may need more if you have a sweet tooth.
– In a hurry? Use frozen ready-prepared jackfruit.

TIP: If you add 2 cups crushed ice or cubes to the blender and blitz with the other ingredients to a slush, you'll have a frozen jackfruit margarita drink. If it's too thick for your liking, thin it with more juice or ice.

JACKFRUIT COCONUT ICE CREAM WITH ROASTED CASHEWS

SERVES: 6 | **PREP:** 20 MINUTES | **FREEZE:** 4–6 HOURS

12 fresh ripe, sweet jackfruit pods (arils), deseeded and sliced

400g/14oz can full-fat coconut milk

1 tbsp maple syrup or agave nectar

3 tbsp cashew nut butter

1 tsp vanilla extract

pinch of sea salt

roasted cashews, for sprinkling

thinly sliced ripe jackfruit, to decorate

This is such a refreshing ice cream on a hot summer's day. If you have an ice cream maker, prepare the jackfruit and coconut purée as described below, then follow the manufacturer's instructions. If you can find a packet of frozen jackfruit, you can substitute it for fresh.

1 Put the ripe jackfruit pods into a blender and blitz until you have a thick, creamy purée.

2 Add the coconut milk, maple syrup, cashew nut butter, vanilla extract and sea salt and blitz again.

3 Pour into a plastic container and cover with cling film (plastic wrap). Freeze for 1–2 hours, then remove from the freezer and stir to break up any ice crystals. Return to the freezer for 2 hours and repeat. Freeze for a further 1–2 hours longer before serving.

4 Serve scooped into bowls, sprinkled with cashews and topped with sliced ripe jackfruit. The ice cream will keep in the freezer for up to 1 month.

OR YOU CAN TRY THIS...

– If you're not vegan, stir in some double (heavy) cream before freezing.
– Set aside half the puréed jackfruit and then swirl into the coconut mixture before freezing.
– Add some diced fresh jackfruit to the mixture before freezing.
– Serve in scoops in ice cream cones.

JACKFRUIT JAM

MAKES: 2KG/4½LB | **PREP:** 20 MINUTES | **COOK:** 30 MINUTES | **COOL:** 15 MINUTES

1kg/2lb 4oz (7 cups) fresh ripe, sweet jackfruit, deseeded and diced
1kg/2lb 4oz preserving or granulated sugar
grated zest and juice of 2 limes
pinch of salt

If you've never made jam before, you'll be surprised at how easy it is. Don't forget to add the lime juice – citrus fruits are very high in pectin, which will help your jam to set. Jackfruit jam has a lovely fragrance and tropical flavour: spread it on bread, toast and muffins or use for filling tarts and cakes or drizzling over desserts.

1 Sterilize some clean jam jars by putting them (lids off) into a very low oven at 110°C, 225°F, gas mark ¼ for 20–30 minutes. Turn the oven off and leave the jars inside until you're ready to fill them.

2 Meanwhile, set aside one-quarter of the jackfruit. Blitz the rest to a smooth purée in a blender.

3 Put the blended and diced jackfruit into a large saucepan with the sugar, lime zest and lime juice. Set over a low heat and keep stirring until the sugar dissolves. Simmer gently for 10 minutes to soften the pieces of jackfruit.

4 Turn up the heat and bring to the boil. Boil rapidly for about 15 minutes, or until the jam reaches setting point. You can test this by using a sugar thermometer (setting point is at 105°C, 220°F), or by dropping a teaspoonful onto a chilled saucer. Push it gently with your finger; if it wrinkles, it's set. If the jam is still a bit runny, boil it for a few more minutes. This jam will be more of a soft set (slightly syrupy and sloppy) than a hard set (set firm).

5 Remove the pan from the heat and set aside to cool for 15 minutes before ladling the jam into the warm sterilized jars. Cover with a wax disc and a jam cover or screw-top lid.

6 Store the jam in a cool, dark place. It will keep for up to 6 months. Once opened, keep the jar in the fridge.

OR YOU CAN TRY THIS...

– Add the seeds of a vanilla pod or 1 teaspoon vanilla paste to the jam as it's cooling.
– Substitute lemon zest and juice for the lime.
– You can use special 'jam sugar', which has added pectin.

SCENTED TROPICAL FRUIT SALAD

SERVES: 6 | **PREP:** 20 MINUTES | **COOK:** 10 MINUTES | **CHILL:** 1 HOUR+

400g/14oz can jackfruit
   in syrup
2 lemongrass stalks, peeled
120ml/4fl oz (½ cup) fresh
   orange juice
2 tbsp coconut sugar or
   soft brown sugar
1 small ripe pineapple
2 passion fruit
1 ripe mango, peeled, stoned
   (pitted) and sliced
200g/7oz (1 cup)
   strawberries, hulled
   and sliced
seeds of ½ pomegranate

We've used canned jackfruit in syrup as a base for this refreshing fruit salad, but if you can find fresh, ripe jackfruit, do try it. Sweet and fragrant, its flavour is reminiscent of other tropical fruits, including mango, papaya, banana and pineapple.

1 Drain the syrup from the jackfruit into a small pan. Bruise the lemongrass by bashing the stalks with a rolling pin and add to the pan with the orange juice and sugar. Set over a low heat and stir until the sugar dissolves. Bring to the boil and boil for 1 minute, then reduce the heat and simmer for 5 minutes, or until slightly reduced. Remove from the heat and set aside to cool and infuse with the flavour and scent of the lemongrass.

2 Peel the pineapple and cut in half lengthways. Cut out the central hard core and then cut the fruit horizontally into chunks. Transfer to a large shallow serving bowl.

3 Cut the passion fruit in half and, with a small spoon, scoop out the seeds and juice into the serving bowl.

4 Add the canned jackfruit, mango and strawberry slices and spoon the syrup over the top. Chill in the fridge for at least 1 hour. Serve scattered with pomegranate seeds.

OR YOU CAN TRY THIS...
– Sprinkle with strips of toasted coconut and serve with coconut ice cream.
– Serve with sprigs of fresh mint.
– Instead of lemongrass, use ½ teaspoon grated fresh root ginger.
– Add some lime juice and finely shredded lime or orange zest.
– You can add almost any fruit. Try papaya (pawpaw), lychees, orange segments, kiwi fruit, melon, peaches and raspberries.

SWEET JACKFRUIT FRITTERS WITH TOASTED COCONUT

SERVES: 4 | **PREP:** 20 MINUTES | **COOK:** 10–15 MINUTES

12 fresh ripe sweet
    jackfruit pods (arils)
100g/3½oz (1 cup) plain
    (all-purpose) flour
50g/2oz (½ cup) rice flour
1 tsp baking powder
¼ tsp ground cardamom
pinch of grated nutmeg
200ml/7fl oz (scant 1 cup)
    cold water
vegetable or groundnut
    (peanut) oil, for
    deep-frying
caster (superfine) sugar,
    for dusting
finely shredded zest of
    1 lime
200g/7oz (scant 1 cup)
    coconut yoghurt
toasted coconut flakes,
    for sprinkling

Crisp and golden on the outside and fragrant and juicy inside, these jackfruit fritters make a great dessert. They are very popular in Kerala in southern India, where jackfruit trees grow wild. If you're short on time, look for frozen packs of prepared sweet jackfruit pods.

1 Prepare the jackfruit, wearing gloves to protect your hands against any sticky latex. Lubricate the knife with some vegetable oil and take a pod (aril) and make a slit along one side. Cut out the seed (pit) and discard it, along with its rubbery skin. Rinse the jackfruit pods under running water and pat dry with kitchen paper (paper towels).

2 Make the batter: put the flours, baking powder and spices in a bowl. Stir in the water and beat with a whisk until the batter is smooth and creamy.

3 Heat the oil to 180°C, 350°F in a deep heavy saucepan. You can use a sugar thermometer to check the temperature.

4 Dip the jackfruit pods into the batter, a few at a time so as not to overcrowd the pan, and lower them gently into the hot oil. Deep-fry until golden all over, turning the fritters once. Remove with a slotted spoon and drain on kitchen paper, then sprinkle with caster sugar. Keep warm while you cook the remaining fritters.

5 Stir the lime zest into the coconut yoghurt and place a spoonful on each serving plate. Add the jackfruit fritters and serve, sprinkled with toasted coconut.

OR YOU CAN TRY THIS...
– Add some ground turmeric or cinnamon to the fritter batter.
– Serve with mango sorbet or coconut ice cream.

JACKFRUIT SMOOTHIE BOWL

SERVES: 4 | **PREP:** 10 MINUTES

450g/1lb (3 cups) fresh ripe, sweet jackfruit, deseeded and chopped

2 ripe bananas

1 ripe mango, peeled, stoned (pitted) and chopped

seeds from 6 cardamom pods

360ml/12fl oz (1½ cups) almond or coconut milk

200g/7oz (2 cups) blueberries or raspberries

4 tbsp shredded coconut

4 tbsp pumpkin seeds

4 tbsp chopped pistachios

A smoothie bowl makes a delicious and filling breakfast and it's ready in a few minutes. All you have to do is blitz everything in the blender and top with fruit, nuts and seeds. You can also make the smoothie in advance and chill in the fridge for up to 1 hour before sprinkling with the toppings.

1 Put the jackfruit, peeled bananas, mango, cardamom seeds and plant milk in a blender or food chopper and blitz until thick and smooth.

2 Divide the smoothie mixture between 4 bowls and top with the fresh berries, shredded coconut, pumpkin seeds and pistachios. Eat immediately.

OR YOU CAN TRY THIS...

– Use coconut water instead of almond or coconut milk.
– Add some lime juice to counteract the sweetness of the fruit.
– Make the smoothie less sweet by adding some fresh spinach leaves, kale or celery.
– Top with blackberries, sliced strawberries or kiwi fruit.
– Sprinkle with chopped almonds, walnuts or toasted pine nuts.

KERALAN JACKFRUIT LASSI

SERVES: 2 | **PREP:** 10 MINUTES

4 saffron strands
1 tbsp hot milk
150g/5oz (1 cup) fresh ripe, sweet jackfruit, deseeded and chopped
10 ice cubes
240g/8oz (1 cup) Greek or coconut yoghurt
¼ tsp ground cardamom
1 tbsp agave nectar or maple syrup
2 tsp rose water (optional)
chopped pistachios, for sprinkling

On a hot summer day, a long glass of fruity lassi is soothing and cooling. The flavour of this refreshing drink is even better and more authentic if you grind the seeds of 4 cardamom pods in a pestle and mortar rather than using ready-ground cardamom.

1 Add the saffron to the hot milk and set aside until cold.

2 Blitz the jackfruit and ice cubes in a blender until puréed. Add the yoghurt, saffron milk and cardamom and blitz until smooth. If the lassi is too thick for your liking, you can thin it with some water, milk or coconut milk.

3 Taste before adding the agave nectar or maple syrup – you may need less or more, depending on whether you have a sweet tooth. Stir in the rose water (if using).

4 Pour into 2 tall glasses and sprinkle with chopped pistachios. Drink immediately.

OR YOU CAN TRY THIS...
– Add some diced mango or banana.
– Use chopped almonds instead of pistachios.

JACKFRUIT BANANA BREAD

MAKES: 1 X 450G/1LB LOAF | **PREP:** 15 MINUTES | **COOK:** 1 HOUR

125g/4oz (½ cup) butter, plus extra for greasing
175g/6oz (scant 1 cup) soft light brown sugar
2 medium free-range eggs
3 large ripe bananas, mashed
150g/5oz (1¼ cups) coarsely chopped walnuts
225g/8oz (2¼ cups) self-raising (self-rising) flour, plus extra for dusting
½ tsp bicarbonate of soda (baking soda)
½ tsp salt
½ tsp grated nutmeg
½ tsp ground cinnamon
225g/8oz (1½ cups) fresh ripe, sweet jackfruit, deseeded and diced

Banana bread is very popular in many islands in the Caribbean, and sometimes ripe jackfruit is added to the batter before cooking. If you can't get hold of fresh ripe jackfruit, use canned instead; simply drain it and discard the syrup before stirring into the banana mixture.

1 Preheat the oven to 180°C, 350°F, gas mark 4. Line a buttered 450g (1lb) loaf tin (pan) with baking parchment.

2 Cream together the butter and sugar in a large bowl. Beat in the eggs, one at a time, and then mix in the mashed banana and walnuts.

3 Sift in the flour and bicarbonate of soda, add the salt and spices and fold in gently. Dust the jackfruit with a little flour and add it to the mixture, distributing it evenly throughout.

4 Spoon the mixture into the prepared loaf tin and level the top. Bake for about 1 hour until risen and golden brown. You can test if it's cooked by inserting a thin skewer into the centre. The banana bread is ready when the skewer comes out clean.

5 Leave the loaf to cool in the tin for 10 minutes, then turn out onto a wire rack. Once cool, cut into slices to serve. It will keep well, wrapped in foil, for up to 5 days.

OR YOU CAN TRY THIS...
– Add a few drops of vanilla extract.
– Add some ground cloves, ginger or allspice.
– Add some poppy seeds.
– Stir in some raisins or sultanas (golden raisins).
– Sprinkle with shredded coconut flakes before baking.

SPICY JACKFRUIT CHUTNEY

MAKES: APPROX. 2KG/4LB | **PREP:** 20 MINUTES | **COOK:** 1–1¼ HOURS

1 tsp fenugreek seeds
6 tbsp sunflower oil
1 tbsp cumin seeds
2 tbsp black mustard seeds
2.5cm/1in piece fresh root
    ginger, peeled and diced
5 garlic cloves, crushed
2 red chillies, diced
1 large onion, diced
450g/1lb (3 cups) fresh ripe,
    sweet jackfruit, deseeded
    and diced
1.5kg/3lb tomatoes, skinned
    and chopped
450g/1lb (2 cups)
    granulated sugar
300ml/½ pint (1¼ cups)
    malt vinegar
1 tsp salt

This chutney is pungent, spicy and aromatic, with a hint of tropical sweetness from the jackfruit. Try not to eat it all straight away – if you can bear to put it in a cupboard for two or three weeks before opening it will taste even better. Once opened, store in the fridge.

1 Toast the fenugreek seeds in a dry frying pan (skillet) over a medium heat for 1–2 minutes, stirring occasionally. Remove from the pan and set aside to cool.

2 Heat the oil in a large, heavy-based saucepan set over a low heat and cook the cumin and mustard seeds and toasted fenugreek seeds for 2–3 minutes. Stir in the ginger, garlic and chillies and cook for a further 2–3 minutes.

3 Reduce the heat and add the onion, jackfruit, tomatoes and sugar and simmer gently for 15 minutes, stirring occasionally to dissolve the sugar. Stir in the vinegar and salt and simmer gently until the mixture thickens to a syrupy, chutney-like consistency without any liquid – this might take anything from 40 minutes to 1 hour. Stir the chutney regularly to prevent it catching and burning on the bottom of the pan.

4 Meanwhile, sterilize some clean jars by putting them (lids off) into a very low oven at 110°C, 225°F, gas mark ¼ for about 20 minutes. Turn the oven off and leave the jars inside until you're ready to fill them.

5 Ladle the hot chutney into the sterilized jars and half-screw on the lids. When they are cool, tighten the lids and store in a cool, dark place for up to 3 months.

OR YOU CAN TRY THIS...
– Add some diced pumpkin, red (bell) pepper, or apples.
– Use 2 teaspoons chilli powder instead of fresh chillies.
– Use brown sugar instead of white.
– Add some ground turmeric, cardamom, coriander and cloves.

SEEDY JACKFRUIT RAITA

SERVES: 6 | **PREP:** 10 MINUTES | **COOK:** 8-10 MINUTES

3 tbsp unsalted butter
  or ghee
150g/5oz (1 cup) fresh ripe,
  sweet jackfruit, deseeded
  and diced
2 tbsp soft brown sugar
480g/16oz (2 cups) Greek
  yoghurt
1 tsp red chilli powder
1 tsp roasted cumin seeds
a handful of mint, finely
  chopped
a handful of coriander
  (cilantro), finely chopped
1 tsp black mustard seeds
8 curry leaves
fine sea salt, to taste

A gently spiced yoghurt-based raita is a cooling and refreshing accompaniment to curries and intensely flavoured hot dishes. Alternatively, it makes a delicious dip for vegetable crudités. You will need to use a thick, creamy yoghurt – the full-fat Greek sort is best.

1 Melt 2 tablespoons of the butter or ghee in a small frying pan (skillet) set over a medium to high heat. Add the jackfruit and turn it in the butter. Sprinkle with the brown sugar and cook for 8–10 minutes, turning occasionally, until golden brown and starting to caramelize. Set aside to cool.

2 Beat the yoghurt in a bowl until thick and creamy. Stir in the chilli powder, cumin seeds, mint and coriander. Season to taste with salt. Stir in the cooled caramelized jackfruit.

3 Melt the remaining butter or ghee in a small clean frying pan set over a medium heat. When it's hot, add the mustard seeds and curry leaves and cook for 10–15 seconds, or until they start to crackle. Remove from the heat and drizzle immediately over the raita.

OR YOU CAN TRY THIS...
– Use pineapple instead of jackfruit.
– Add some diced cucumber.
– Use fresh red or green chillies instead of chilli powder.
– Add some garam masala, ground cumin or grated fresh root ginger.
– Squeeze some lime juice over the top.

JACKFRUIT, RASPBERRY & COCONUT MUFFINS

MAKES: 12 | **PREP:** 15 MINUTES | **COOK:** 20-25 MINUTES

300g/10oz (3 cups) self-raising (self-rising) flour

60g/2oz (¾ cup) desiccated coconut, plus extra for sprinkling

175g/6oz (scant 1 cup) light muscovado sugar

1 tsp ground cinnamon

60g/2oz (4 tbsp) butter, melted

180ml/6fl oz (¾ cup) kefir or natural yoghurt

2 tbsp milk

2 medium free-range eggs, beaten

a few drops of vanilla extract

150g/5oz (1 cup) fresh ripe, sweet jackfruit, deseeded and diced

60g/2oz (½ cup) raspberries

Eat these fruity muffins at any time of day. You can even have them for dessert with a dollop of ice cream or crème fraîche and some fresh berries.

1 Preheat the oven to 180°C, 350°F, gas mark 4 and line a 12-hole muffin tin (pan) with paper cases.

2 Sift the flour into a large mixing bowl and add the coconut, sugar and cinnamon. Mix well and make a hollow in the centre.

3 In a separate bowl or jug, mix together the butter, kefir or yoghurt, milk, eggs and vanilla extract. Pour into the flour mixture and stir until everything is combined and smooth. Gently stir through the jackfruit and raspberries.

4 Divide the batter between the paper cases and sprinkle some coconut on top. Bake for 20–25 minutes until risen and golden brown. Cool on a wire rack.

5 Eat warm or cold. The muffins will keep well in an airtight container for up to 3 days in the fridge, or you can freeze them for up to 1 month.

OR YOU CAN TRY THIS...
– Add a mashed banana to the batter.
– Use blackberries or blueberries instead of raspberries.
– Go tropical and substitute pineapple or mango for the berries.
– Dust the cooked muffins with icing (confectioner's) sugar.

INDEX

10 9 8 7 6 5 4 3 2 1

Published in 2020 by Ebury Press an imprint of Ebury Publishing,
20 Vauxhall Bridge Road,
London SW1V 2SA

Ebury Press is part of the Penguin Random House group of companies
whose addresses can be found at global.penguinrandomhouse.com

Penguin
Random House
UK

Design: Louise Evans
Photography: Joff Lee
Food Styling: Mari Williams
Prop Styling: Rachel Vere
Editor: Camilla Ackley

Heather Thomas has asserted her right to be identified as the author of this work
in accordance with the Copyright, Designs and Patents Act 1988

This edition first published by Ebury Press in 2020

www.penguin.co.uk

A CIP catalogue record for this book is available from the British Library

ISBN 9781529107388

Printed and bound in China by Toppan Leefung

MIX
Paper from
responsible sources
FSC® C018179